OUR ONE WORD

CREATING SPIRITUAL
JOY AND DEPTH

MARTHA JOHNSON
BOURLAKAS

Church Publishing
NEW YORK

Unless otherwise noted, the Scripture quotations contained herein are from the New Revised Standard Version Bible, copyright © 1989 by the Division of Christian Education of the National Council of Churches of Christ in the U.S.A. Used by permission. All rights reserved.

Church Publishing
19 East 34th Street
New York, NY 10016
www.churchpublishing.org

Cover logo by Cherilyn Colbert
Cover design by Jennifer Kopec, 2Pug Design
Typeset by Rose Design

Library of Congress Cataloging-in-Publication Data

A record of this book is available from the Library of Congress.

ISBN-13: 978-1-64065-019-0 (pbk.)
ISBN-13: 978-1-64065-020-6 (ebook)

Printed in the United States of America

For Mark, Hannah, Sarah and Elizabeth
With gratitude and love for the stories we live and share

For Margie and Martha Lois,
The women who will forever define me

Contents

Introduction 1

How This Works 9

Crooked Path Prayer 15

Beginnings 17

Hope 25

Fear 31

Peace 37

Joy 43

Spirit 51

Wonder 61

Pickling 67

Abundance 75

Change 85

Red 91

Feast 99

Night 107

Laugh 115

Beauty 125

Movement 131

Name 137

Cairns 145

Bread 155

Heaven 163

Boundaries 169

Perfect. 175

Wilderness 183

Surrender 191

Word 199

Stories 203

Introduction

In the beginning was the Word, and the Word was with God, and the Word was God.

—John 1:1

I came to *Our One Word* unwittingly. No offense to Jesus, but before *Our One Word*, I was embarrassed to be identified as a *Christian writer* or a *Christian speaker*. I had to be more hip, smarter than that. Christian-Writer-Speaker-Woman carries her Bible in her hand and wears a perpetual smile on her face. CWSW does not roll her eyes, dig through laundry for a clean t-shirt, drink much strong coffee, wear jeans with holes, talk about sex, listen to Kendrick Lamar. She is not me. But then I realized I was pigeonholing myself in the same ways I criticize others for doing. Assuming that being a Christian means thinking, dressing, behaving in narrow ways. Assuming that faith cannot exist alongside intelligence and creativity. Assuming that God's community of believers is boxed in, with a low ceiling of wooden slats nailed too close together and no breathing space for difference.

When I started listening to the stories and experiences of so many other women, I realized this seemingly contradictory mashup was exactly the point. Jesus did not command One Way to live this life, which makes things complicated, and God knows we don't have time for extra complications right now. Black-and-white rules are much easier to command and follow, both for ourselves and each other. However, the so-called rules of the Christian journey are striking in their non-rulish-ness. They open up a lot of grey questions and invite more questions than solutions: Do not judge. Forgive wrongdoing. Act and speak for the marginalized and powerless. Love, love, love.

Kudos to Jesus for these important ideas and thoughts, but how do we actually turn these ideas into reality, a new way to live in the midst of all we do already? Even if we wrangle ourselves and/or our children to attend worship, we are exhausted by noon, having taught Sunday school, sung in the choir, met with the Vestry, doled out cookies at coffee hour. If we do find peace in our worship, we have classes and work and chemotherapy and parent-teacher conferences and meetings and dentist appointments and exercise and dirty dishes in the sink. *Our One Word* offers a chance to settle, be with ourselves, be with each other, be with the Word of God. *Our One Word* is a way of listening to each other, a chance for practicing creativity, a space for the presence of the Holy Spirit.

A kind of spiritual happy hour, *Our One Word* is a time for women to come together with no obligations, no committee assignments, no committee reports, no homework, no cost, no guilt. We sit together, share food like popcorn and chocolate that requires no cooking or preparation, drink wine or coffee or soda, and look with intent at one word each week. We discuss how each word is or is not at work in our lives at the particular moment. We view the word from all sides—etymology, meaning, how the word is used in spiritual writing, where and how it appears in literature and culture. We take a creative approach to each word that may involve writing, coloring, designing. Then we eat and talk some more.

Through this process of sitting together, eating, drinking, praying, talking, writing, laughing, coloring, we slow down and pay attention to the words and stories of each other's lives. We become more aware of God's abundant love and wisdom that exists, right along with the darkness, both in our world and within ourselves. When we are attuned to that wisdom, we start living into it. We begin listening better to each other. We begin to see hope in the brushstrokes instead of struggling with the entire painting. By breaking down the elements of the art, we move, more gently, through judgment, guilt, shame, heartbreak, disease, to joy, laughter, wisdom, nourishment, peace, love.

Franciscan priest Fr. Richard Rohr said, "The history of almost every religion begins with one massive misperception, making a fatal distinction between the sacred and the profane. . . . Your task is to find the good, the true, and the beautiful in everything, even and most especially the problematic. The bad is never strong enough to counteract the good."[1]

Our One Word is an attempt to work away from the misperception that we must, in order to be spiritual people, separate the sacred and profane. It is one method of plowing a more sacred path directly through this gnarly, brush-filled landscape. A method of understanding that contradiction exists at every human turn. Profound destruction and explosive beauty. Vengeful hatred and soul-stirring love. *Our One Word* seeks to incorporate more of the holy into the difficult world that is right before us, so we tune ourselves to God's green abundance, rather than

---

1. Adapted from Richard Rohr, *Franciscan Mysticism: I AM That Which I Am Seeking*, disc 1. (Center for Action and Contemplation, 2012), CD/MP3 download; *Eager to Love: The Alternative Way of Francis of Assisi* (Cincinnati: Franciscan Media, 2014), 10; and "Franciscan Mysticism," unpublished talk, April 12, 2012.

the dry, crackly landscape of scarce time, money, health, peace, joy. *Our One Word* is a beginning, an opening to our deeper connection with ourselves and each other in a fractured time. I pray these words help us question as much as we answer, grow from each other's stories, give us time for authentic hospitality, and open space for the presence and power of the Holy Spirit.

It can be difficult to talk about Christianity in our current, or maybe any, climate. In this moment, as in all moments of history, the attention-seeking Christians holler loudest so that everyone around has no choice but to listen and look. I grew up in the Bible Belt of East Tennessee where a vocal group always tried to abscond with Christianity and chain it to a chair in a dark room where only the Select could visit. Classmates of mine repeated the rules of their churches and parents: *If you are not dunked in a pool, you are not truly baptized. If you drink alcohol, you will roast in hell. If you do not get saved, you are not truly a Christian.* (I never thought I would long for a return to those simple arguments, but here we are.)

As panic and anxiety intensify in our world, it seems that some, particularly white, Christian belts tighten, exclude even more, turn hateful and intolerant. *Christians must only vote for certain candidates. Christians must only listen and talk to people with certain, similar beliefs. Christians only love other white Christians.* I understand the way this exclusive, mean version of Christianity makes non-believers or decent Christians furious. I can understand at times wanting to discard the entire Christian story, throw it in a box with all the other basement junk, and drop it off at Goodwill or maybe take it straight to the landfill to rot with the old Pampers. In the end, the white belt will never ever, under any circumstances, be right, stylish, or attractive. Jesus never ever instructed us to hate or exclude. Quite the opposite. He instructed us, not even politely, to crawl on up out of our dark, dirt holes and start listening to each other, talking to each other, fighting for those voices that have weakened or evaporated.

Then there is the other side. Those who disregard Christianity or other faiths as outmoded, anti-science, irrelevant to the times. These assumptions can become as superior and exclusive as the opposite side. *It's enough to be a good person, to do good in the world. I don't need a tired old male narrative to figure out myself in relationship to this world. I have botany, psychology, meditation, philosophy, nutrition, sociology, mathematics.* I meditate most every day, check in regularly with my therapist, and read everything I can about recipes and healing foods, so I get this perspective (except for the math part). As critical as these practices and sciences are, I believe our human offerings and interactions can also be what hurt us most. With our human progression and regression comes anxiety, frustration, competition, frenetic pace, strict pigeonholing. If I sit for just five minutes with my spinach-chia-strawberry smoothie, I start to question and wallow.

Why do these chia seeds lodge in my teeth? What of soul mysteries? How do I name my yearning for something more complex, deeper than what humanity has created? What is the something beyond humanity or science in the eyes of my dogs, my relationship with my children, the green of the trees lining the James River? What is the wisdom of the Holy Spirit deep within my well-worn body and heart? And how do I talk about these questions in a fact-based world with other people, without sounding like a nutjob-science-denier or a humorless Bible-thumper?

These obvious questions of faith and religion have kept people on their toes forever. I have to make myself stop. Sip through the straw, stop questioning for a change, and listen for the Holy Spirit.

The Christian narrative refuses to be easily distilled. One group of people does not get to own the Christian story, because it is much broader than any human can conceive. As a mother of a young adult with autism, I have learned it is both inaccurate and harmful to assume the spectrum is narrow. Wild creativity, critical thinking, difficult questioning, thirsty drought, fertile woods—all of this is not some deviance from the story, but critical to its composition. In the end, what kind of God would be so predictable, so simplistic? The narrative about what it means to live in the Holy Spirit is neither succinctly composed nor quickly read.

Sometimes it seems impossible to say the good can overcome the bad. In plain sight, shootings and cancer and hurricanes storm around us like bald-headed turkey buzzards circling a dead rat or deer in the woods. The words of the Holy Spirit and the world have helped me wake up and get moving and that is our first step. Our choice is to lie there and wait for the swoop, or start listening, moving, grasping for the words of the Holy Spirit. These words have also taught me that the sky is vast. When we sit with each other and with the words of our lives, we start to hear blue-sky stories of hope that enable us to return home—whatever, wherever that home may be.

How This Works

The method in these pages is my framework for *Our One Word* workshops and retreats. Many participants and I have found these words and resources to be remarkable catalysts for story-sharing, problem-solving, and action. I intend for this book to be a guide for your own *Our One Word* sessions, groups, and retreats. This is all intended to be a **beginning** to a larger, deeper, more meaningful conversation within ourselves, with each other, and with the Holy Spirit. Some days, all we can do is begin.

Although each chapter is not exactly the same, the general, consistent structure is that of a story, with a beginning, middle, and end. With this structure, I want us to reflect on our own life stories—the ones that may have already ended and the ones that are still unsolved mysteries. We begin with as complete a definition of the word as possible from the comprehensive online *Oxford Dictionary*. Although we all generally know what words mean, it's interesting to consider how definitions can become distorted when they are not contemplated. We may miss the alternate meanings or nuances. Different meanings can point us to different understandings.

After the definitions, we look at spiritual sources for the word. I come from a Christian perspective, so I include references to the word from the Bible. Although I am less informed about sources from other religious traditions, I try to look to those sources too, when possible, in hopes that we expand our learning from and communication with each other. Although I include specific Bible verses, I do not assume that these verses are ever taken out of historical context or removed from the limitations of human interpretation. I do assume that the most primary messages of the Bible and the life of Jesus are that life is not meant to be easy or simple. Despite this, *because of this*, we must love, love each other. We desperately need each other.

After the spiritual sources, we look at the use of the word within our culture—in literature, poetry, song, plays, movies, sometimes even commercials. As God, the Word, became flesh and lived among us in Jesus Christ, so do our own words and stories live and walk and work in *this* life, in *this* culture, with all its creative chaos and fleshly imperfection. In *this* world, not some soft, pillowy escape, we must seek the grace and truth in each other that mirror the eternal grace and truth of God. In the symbolic reciprocity of words in the Spirit and words in the world, I pray we experience God's presence, especially in the most human of moments—in our arguments, in our illnesses, in our loneliness, in the dark alleyways of our lives.

All of the suggested activities are intended to fuse creativity with internal and spiritual questioning and seeking, but I am flexible (at least in some areas). Heck, I am not even sitting there with you. Where I suggest writing, go ahead and draw. Where I suggest drawing, go sit in the dirt of your garden and map some stones. The goal is to push yourself creatively—to work away from saying, *I am not a writer* or *I am not an artist*—into an awareness that we are all creative beings in some way. Creating and recreating is the joy of the Holy Spirit. She doesn't care if we draw with stick figures, dance, or sprinkle glitter. Within *Our One Word*, you have time. No one will grade your work, judge your work, send it to your mother, unless, of course, **you** want to send it to your mother. Try these exercises and let me know how they go.

We end each word chapter with a prayer, many times from *Women's Uncommon Prayers*, an Episcopal source written by and for women. Truthfully, there are times that *Our One Word* group discussions are so rich and lively that I forget to pray in the end before it's time for everyone to go eat dinner. It works as both an excuse and a truth to claim that the conversation, the laughter, the tears, the forgetting is all an important form of prayer. We sit together, exposing ourselves with full vulnerability to God. The ending prayers in these chapters, which my editor, Nancy, has made sure I have not forgotten, are intended to be the reflective prayer of each word and session. The way we balance conversation with quiet questions: *Where was God in this moment, this story, this lifetime? Where am I with God?*

Our One Word should lead you to ask many questions of each other and yourself. One question I ask groups over and over after each session is, *What surprised you?* I want to know if there is something about the word, quotation, or activity that catches you off guard or leads you to something new. The surprises of the Holy Spirit sometimes leave us basking in a soft bath of multicolored confetti. Other times, She leaves us flat on our asses, scraped up, scrambling to get off the unforgiving concrete. If we pay attention to the anger, confusion, joy of even a small surprise, we can awaken, change, act.

I am beyond grateful for the time you spend with this book and with each other. If you have creative, positive suggestions or observations about *Our One Word*, I would love to hear. If you have complaints, please share those behind my back. Even though age has helped me better accept criticism, I'm still not very good at it. My goal is that our words and stories strengthen our connectivity and awareness of shared common experiences. We know that this connectivity and awareness are not static. Words and stories must adapt, change, and grow, as will this method. I pray we recognize that difference is no more threatening than sameness and that our differences define us as children of God. I hope *Our One Word* is a means to recognize God's image within all of us and the wise power we have to do what is right, to become more, to become better.

Crooked Path Prayer

I talk funny. Not as funny as some of y'all do, but my flat
    Southern *I*'s may fall crooked on some of your ears.
I grew up at the foot of the Appalachian Mountains,
    where we learned from an early age that crooked
    is good.

I'm not talking about the raving racist crooked that hides
    in dark hollers, but the crooked of muddy mountain
    trails that teach us to be aware and pay attention.
Attention to flowers, to the wind, to our direction.

I pray my Southern voice might keep you aware of the
    beauty of your own crooked, mountainous path.
Aware that slow is good—especially when it comes to
    growing a camellia or making a coconut cake.

Let me say that one more time: Slow is good.

I pray that while you read this book, you embrace your
    belovedness as a wandering child of God.

Both lost and found.

Amen.

Beginnings

Definitions

Noun:

The point in time or space at which something begins.

The first part or earliest stage of something.

The background or origins of a person or organization.

Beginning of *Beginning*—Ha!

What words and emotions come to mind when you hear the word *beginning, beginnings,* or *begin*?

Throughout the Torah of Judaism is the maxim *All beginnings are hard*, with the explanation that enduring these difficult beginnings leads to transformation. What are examples of this truth?

Genesis 1:1

In the beginning when God created the heavens and the earth . . .

Psalm 111:10

The fear of the Lord is the beginning of wisdom;
all those who practice it have a good understanding.
His praise endures forever.

Wisdom of Solomon 6:17

The beginning of wisdom is the most sincere desire for instruction, and concern for instruction is love of her . . .

1 John 2:24

Let what you heard from the beginning abide in you. If what you heard from the beginning abides in you, then you will abide in the Son and in the Father.

ooo

. . . to begin a new life afresh . . . I replied: we must become somebody who seeks and finds God in all things and at all times, in all places, in all company and in all ways.

—MEISTER ECKHART (c. 1260–1327/8),[1]

CHRISTIAN MYSTIC

---

1. Meister Eckhart, *Selected Writings*, trans. Oliver Davies (London: Penguin Books, 1994), 43–44.

A mother is always the beginning. She is how things begin.

—AMY TAN, *THE BONESETTER'S DAUGHTER*

You've got a chance to start out all over again. A new place, new people, new sights. A clean slate. See, you can be anything you want with a fresh start.

—ANNIE PROULX, *THE SHIPPING NEWS*

I keep turning over new leaves, and spoiling them, as I used to spoil my copybooks; and I make so many beginnings there never will be an end. (Jo March)

—LOUISA MAY ALCOTT, *LITTLE WOMEN*

For it is only by accepting and solving our problems that we can **begin** to get right with ourselves and with the world about us, and with Him who presides over us all.

—ALCOHOLICS ANONYMOUS, *STEP TWELVE*

Every new beginning comes from some other beginning's end.

—SENECA

When we consider *beginning*, we invoke possibility and transformation. No matter what the dark night brings, every morning when we arise, each time we celebrate the Eucharistic feast with the body and blood of Christ, every Easter, we begin again.

> What have been the significant beginnings of your life?
>
> How have those beginnings transformed you?
>
> Are there ways you experience *endings* differently as a result of that transformation?
>
> What are the identifying marks of the many new *you*s that have been born?
>
> What are ways you have guided others in their beginnings?

Now is a good time to listen to Semisonic's song "Closing Time," with a nod to Seneca, from 1998.

Ending

Eastering[2]

It was early in my Eastering that day I looked within.
    Shroud cloths lay discarded round me,
    Mute evidence—marking end of real time
    And new beginnings.

Now I stood
    Naked
    before the tomb of who I'd tried to be,
    of who I thought I was.
And tasted the bitter fact I was no longer *me*.

That diligent, industrious, ever-busy me
    saw her fibrous web of self-deceit torn away
    piece by painful piece.
Each piece held up for mocking,
    flogging, self-derision

---

2. Elizabeth Rankin Geitz, Ann Smith, Marjorie A. Burke, eds., *Women's Uncommon Prayers: Our Lives Revealed, Nurtured, Celebrated* (Harrisburg, PA: Morehouse Publishing, 2000), 303.

By a self who knows her own truth—
Each tattered shroud
     mocked for the flimsy mask
     each had always been.

It has been insidious.
Shroud upon shroud,
     layer after layer,
     year after year.
Muffling me,
Entangling me,
Until that Holy Saturday I gasped for breath
     God's Breath
     Holy Breath
Praying her inspiration to fill my soul.

I then entombed myself with proper care and purpose
     until the sound of rolling stone
     brought me to reality.
Then I fell against my yesterdays,
     mourning and beating my breast
     at the falling of each winding cloth,
For each proclaimed mask of the person who would
     never again
     be *me*.

When I awoke I was empty-tombed.
God had drawn me into Resurrection
    reluctantly, fearfully.

All I could hear was God's soft voice, asking me to yield.
    In giving my obedience to her will I find myself
    Rising free from tattered shrouds
    Rising free from fear
    Rising free from falseness,
    As I yield.

Arisen I now awake revealed.
    Naked, vulnerable,
    No protective masks separating me from thee.

My tomb lies empty in my Eastering
    As I move to share Jesus' Resurrection reality.

—The Rev. Diane Moore,

Women's Uncommon Prayers

Hope

Definitions

Noun:

A feeling of expectation and desire for a particular thing to happen.

A person or thing that may help or save someone.

Grounds for believing that something good may happen.

A feeling of trust.

Verb:

Want something to happen or be the case.

Beginning

List the words, thoughts, emotions you associate with the word *hope*.

What are the ways *hope* has, or has not, been active in your life this week?

Hope can be distinguished from other psychological vehicles, such as self-efficacy and optimism. . . . In contrast to both self-efficacy and optimism, people with hope have both the will and the pathways and strategies necessary to achieve their goals.

—Scott Barry Kaufman, PhD,
Psychology Today (online)

Havel had said that people struggling for independence wanted money and recognition from other countries; they wanted more criticism of the Soviet empire from the West and more diplomatic pressure. But Havel had said that they were things they **wanted**; the only thing they **needed** was hope. Not that pie in the sky stuff, not a preference for optimism over pessimism, but rather an "orientation of the spirit." The kind of hope that creates a willingness to position oneself in a hopeless place and be a witness, that allows one to believe in a better future, even in the face of abusive power. That kind of hope makes one strong.

—Bryan Stevenson, *Just Mercy*
(emphasis added),
writing about Vaclav Havel,
First President of the Czech Republic,
1993–2003

Have you had times of feeling little or no hope? If so, what helped you the most during those times?

In those experiences, how did your relationship with God, the Gospel of Jesus, or your faith sustain you?

Considering the state of politics, job losses, troubling weather patterns, rise of overdoses, and other factors of society, many express increased feelings of hopelessness. What are specific ways the Christian narrative can guide us in being present for people who have lost hope?

Psalm 39:7

"And now, O Lord, what do I wait for?
My hope is in you.

> The language of the psalm associates waiting
> and hope.
>
> How have you experienced this association in your
> own life?

Proverbs 13:12

Hope deferred makes the heart sick,
but a desire fulfilled is a tree of life.

> Draw your own Tree of Life. What are the branches
> of hope that sustain you?

Ending

God Is Our Hope

God is our hope and strength,
a very present help in trouble.
Therefore will we not fear, though the earth be moved,

and though the hills be carried into the midst of the sea;

Though the waters thereof rage and swell,

and though the mountains shake at the tempest of the same.

There is a river, the streams whereof make glad the city
of God,

the holy place of the tabernacle of the Most High.

—BOOK OF COMMON PRAYER 1979

Fear

Definitions

Noun:

An unpleasant emotion caused by the threat of danger, pain, or harm.

Verb:

Be afraid of (someone or something) as likely to be dangerous, painful, or harmful.

Archaic:

A mixed feeling of dread and reverence.

Beginning

What are your physical reactions when you hear the word *fear*?

What are thoughts, emotions that come to mind when you read or hear the word?

How do you differentiate between healthy and unhealthy *fear*?

There are 524 references to *fear* in the Bible (bible. oremus.org), so this is not a word easily cast aside. How does *fear* work in our understanding of the Christian narrative?

Matthew 28:1-10

After the sabbath, as the first day of the week was dawning, Mary Magdalene and the other Mary went to see the tomb. And suddenly there was a great earthquake; for an angel of the Lord, descending from heaven, came and rolled back the stone and sat on it. His appearance was like lightning, and his clothing white as snow. For fear of him the guards shook and became like dead men. But the angel said to the women, "Do not be afraid; I know that you are looking for Jesus who was crucified. He is not here; for he has been raised, as he said. Come, see the place where he lay. Then go quickly and tell his disciples, 'He has been raised from the dead, and indeed he is going ahead of you to Galilee; there you will see him.' This is my message for you." So they left the tomb quickly with fear and great joy, and ran to tell his disciples. Suddenly Jesus met them and said, "Greetings!" And they came to him, took hold of his feet, and worshipped him. Then Jesus said to them, "Do not be afraid; go and tell my brothers to go to Galilee; there they will see me."

ooo

Our deepest fear is not that we are inadequate. Our deepest fear is that we are powerful beyond measure. It is our light, not our darkness that most frightens us. We ask ourselves, "Who am I to be brilliant, gorgeous, talented, fabulous?" Actually, who are you not to be? You are a child of God. Your playing small does not serve the world. There is nothing enlightened about shrinking so that other people won't feel insecure around you. We are all meant to shine, as children do. We were born to make manifest the glory of God that is within us. It's not just in some of us; it's in everyone. And as we let our own light shine, we unconsciously give other people permission to do the same. As we are liberated from our own fear, our presence automatically liberates others.

—MARIANNE WILLIAMSON, *A RETURN TO LOVE: REFLECTIONS ON THE PRINCIPLES OF A COURSE IN MIRACLES*

You must do the thing you think you cannot do.

—Eleanor Roosevelt, *You Learn by Living:*
Eleven Keys for a More Fulfilling Life

The enemy is fear. We think it is hate; but, it is fear.

—Mahatma Gandhi

Fear is the path to the Dark Side. Fear leads to anger, anger leads to hate, hate leads to suffering.

—Yoda, *Star Wars Episode I:*
The Phantom Menace

Storytelling becomes central to conquering fear. It's a way of naming and making sense of fear and imagining different routes out. Storytellers expand the consciousness, waken the sleeping self and give their hearers the words and motifs to use for themselves. Jews tell the story of the Exodus each generation to understand the fears they feel at that moment. Stories create new ways of seeing, which lead to new ways of feeling and thinking.

—David Brooks, *New York Times*
editorial, April 3, 2015

Write down ways storytelling and stories have been used to deal with fear in your family of origin, your immediate family, or the tribe you identify as your family. Choose one of those stories to elaborate and share with your group or someone else reading this book. Rewrite your story on pretty paper and save it with other treasures to share one day with your own child, grandchild, niece, nephew, or any child who might cherish your words of strength.

Ending

A Prayer for Today | John Philip Newell

November 9, 2016

Be strong, O my soul,

Be strong this day

To face this moment and feel its pain

To cry with our mothers and weep for our daughters

To stand by our fathers and sons of colour

And defend our true brothers and sisters of the Qu'ran

To serve compassion rather than fear

To invoke wisdom instead of ignorance

To elect humility over false pride
Be strong, O my soul,
Be strong this day
Be strong this day for love.

—HTTP://HEARTBEATJOURNEY.ORG/2016/11/09
/A-PRAYER-FOR-TODAY-JOHN-PHILIP-NEWELL/

Peace

Definitions

Noun:

Freedom from disturbance; tranquility.

Mental or emotional calm.

A state or period in which there is no war or a war has ended.

A treaty agreeing peace between warring states.

The state of being free from civil disorder.

The state of being free from dissension.

A ceremonial handshake or kiss exchanged during a service in some Churches (now usually only in the Eucharist), symbolizing Christian love and unity.

Beginning

What are words, phrases, emotions that come to mind when you hear or see the word *peace*?

List the people, places, things, experiences that bring you peace. What are characteristics or qualities of these people, things that you find peaceful?

How important is peace in our relationships with ourselves, with each other? To what extent should we go to maintain or seek peace?

John 20:19-23

When it was evening on that day, the first day of the week, and the doors of the house where the disciples had met were locked for fear of the Jews, Jesus came and stood among them and said, "Peace be with you." After he said this, he showed them his hands and his side. Then the disciples rejoiced when they saw the Lord. Jesus said to them again, "Peace be with you. As the Father has sent me, so I send you." When he had said this, he breathed on them and said to them, "Receive the Holy Spirit. If you forgive the sins of any, they are forgiven them; if you retain the sins of any, they are retained."

John 14:27

Peace I leave with you; my peace I give to you. I do not give to you as the world gives. Do not let your hearts be troubled, and do not let them be afraid.

Philippians 4:7

And the peace of God, which surpasses all understanding, will guard your hearts and your minds in Christ Jesus.

ooo

This is not learned by flight from the world, nor is it learned by one who runs away from things, who turns his back on the world and flees into the desert. One must learn to find the solitude within wherever or with whomever he may be.

—Meister Eckhart[1]

1. Universal humanitarianism is essential to solve global problems;
2. Compassion is the pillar of world peace;
3. All world religions are already for world peace in this way, as are all humanitarians of whatever ideology;

---

1. Meister Eckhart, from *Whom God Hid Nothing: Sermons, Writings, and Sayings*, ed. David O'Neal, reprint ed. (Boston: New Seeds, 2005), 19.

4. Each individual has a universal responsibility to shape institutions to serve human needs.

—Dalai Lama XIV, *https:// www.dalailama.com/messages /world-peace/a-human -approach-to-world-peace*

Using colored pencils or markers, draw your own personal pathway to peace. What does your path look like? Is it convoluted, swirling, straight? Who are the people along your path? Include and describe the parts of the path most meaningful to you—spiritual, relational, professional, social, cultural, environmental, political, educational, psychological. Share your path with someone and discuss what might have surprised you. Are there places on your path that need a Dead End sign, a Yield sign, a big round green light?

Ending

O God of peace, who has taught us that in returning and rest we shall be saved, in quietness and in confidence shall be our strength: By the might of your Spirit lift us, we pray, to your presence, where we may be still and know that you are God; through Jesus Christ our Lord. Amen.

—Book of Common Prayer

Prayer of St. Francis

Lord, make me an instrument of your peace:
where there is hatred, let me sow love; where there is
    injury, pardon;
where there is doubt, faith;
where there is despair, hope;
where there is darkness, light; and
where there is sadness, joy.
O, God, grant that I may not so much seek to be consoled
    as to console;
to be understood as to understand;
to be loved as to love;
for it is in giving that we receive;
it is in pardoning that we are pardoned;
and it is in dying that we are born to eternal life. Amen.

Joy

Definitions

Noun:

A feeling of great pleasure and happiness.

A thing that causes joy.

Beginning

With some joyful crayons or markers, list the people, places, moments, things that bring you *joy*.

What is the difference between *joy* and *happiness*?

Romans 15:13

May the God of hope fill you with all joy and peace in believing, so that you may abound in hope by the power of the Holy Spirit.

Psalm 16:11

You show me the path of life.

In your presence there is fullness of joy;
in your right hand are pleasures forevermore.

Psalm 30:5

For his anger is but for a moment;
his favour is for a lifetime.
Weeping may linger for the night,
but joy comes with the morning.

Psalm 98:4

Make a joyful noise to the Lord, all the earth;
break forth into joyous song and sing praises.

Luke 2:10

But the angel said to them, "Do not be afraid; for see—I am bringing you good news of great joy for all the people . . ."

John 16:20

Very truly, I tell you, you will weep and mourn, but the world will rejoice; you will have pain, but your pain will turn into joy.

ooo

When you do things from your soul, you feel a river moving in you, a joy.

—RUMI (THIRTEENTH-CENTURY
SUFI POET)

Joy does not simply happen to us. We have to choose joy and keep choosing it every day. It is a choice based on the knowledge that we belong to God and have found in God our refuge and our safety and that nothing, not even death, can take God away from us.

—HENRI J.M. NOUWEN, *BREAD FOR THE JOURNEY*

In my own worst seasons I've come back from the colorless world of despair by forcing myself to look hard, for a long time, at a single glorious thing: a flame of red geranium outside my bedroom window. And then another: my daughter in a yellow dress. And another: the perfect outline of a full, dark sphere behind the crescent moon. Until I learned to be in love with my life again. Like a stroke victim retraining new parts of the brain to grasp lost skills, I have taught myself joy, over and over again.

—BARBARA KINGSOLVER, *HIGH TIDE IN TUCSON:*
ESSAYS FROM NOW OR NEVER

Some of you say, "Joy is greater than sorrow," and others say, "Nay, sorrow is the greater." But I say unto you, they are inseparable. Together they come, and when one sits alone with you at your board, remember that the other is asleep upon your bed.

—KAHLIL GIBRAN, *THE PROPHET*

Consider two themes from the *joy* quotations:

1. the inextricable relationship between *joy* and sorrow
2. *joy* as a choice in our lives

> Which one of these themes speaks to you, has taught you the most about *joy* in your life?

These are great suggestions for finding joy in everyday life from MeiMei Fox on Mindbodygreen.com (full list: *https://www.mindbodygreen.com/0-13874/40-ways-to-practice-joy-every-single-day.html*, May 25, 2014):

> Go barefoot.
>
> Play. Go to a playground and hop on the swings, the slide, and the merry-go-round. Or bust out a board game at home.

Cheerlead someone to greatness. One of the keys to joy is realizing it's not all about you.

Speak to yourself with kindness. Say out loud five times: "I am more than enough." The Dalai Lama once said that not feeling good enough is the great curse of Western culture. Value yourself and others will value you.

Blow bubbles. Remember how enchanting they were when you were a kid?

Spend some reflective time alone. Whether or not you meditate regularly, you can always take a few minutes to move away from others, turn off music, put down your smartphone, and enjoy total silence.

Offer to cook a meal for others. Put love into the food as you prepare it. View it as an act of service.

Look at photos from a vacation you loved. According to research by Stanford professor Jennifer Aaker, focusing on happy memories brings up positive emotions.

Give someone a zerbert. Hug your partner, child, parent, friend in tight, then plant your wet lips on their arm or stomach and blow!

Learn to say *hello*, *goodbye*, and *thank you* in another language.

Download a farting app or buy a whoopee cushion and go to town.

Practice seeing the world in shades of gray. Life isn't black and white. Even those who hurt you are suffering. Reminding yourself of this helps let go of resentments and frustrations.

Have a "NO to-do list" day. Just be.

Snuggle up. Get cozy with a pet, partner, or child. Physical touch releases endorphins that instantly make us feel happier.

Move. Dance, run, twirl, leap, do a somersault or a handstand. Get your heart pumping and your body into action.

Pray. No matter how much you want or imagine yourself to be, you're not in charge. It's a relief, actually.

Ending

The Vespers Psalm, I Will Sing to the Lord

O Lord, you are my portion and my cup;* it is you who
uphold my lot.

My boundaries enclose a pleasant land;* indeed, I have a
goodly heritage.

I will bless the Lord who gives me counsel;* my heart
teaches me, night after night.

I have set the Lord always before me;* because he is at my
right hand I shall not fall.

My heart, therefore, is glad, and my spirit rejoices;* my
body also shall rest in hope.

For you will not abandon me to the grave,* nor let your
holy one see the Pit.

You will show me the path of life;* in your presence there
is fullness of joy, and in

Your right hand are pleasures for evermore.

—FROM *THE DIVINE HOURS* (*VOL. 3*):
PRAYERS FOR SPRINGTIME, BY PHYLLIS TICKLE,
THE VESPERS PSALM, JAN. 17, 2006, P. 17

Spirit

Definitions

Noun:

The non-physical part of a person which is the seat of emotions and character; the soul.

The non-physical part of a person regarded as their true self and as capable of surviving.

The non-physical part of a person manifested as an apparition after their death; a ghost.

A supernatural being.

The prevailing or typical quality, mood, or attitude of a person, group, or period of time.

A person identified with their most prominent quality or with their role in a group or movement.

A person's mood or attitude.

The quality of courage, energy, and determination.

The real meaning or the intention behind something as opposed to its strict verbal interpretation.

Strong distilled alcoholic drink such as brandy, whisky, gin, or rum.

A volatile liquid, especially a fuel, prepared by distillation.

A solution of volatile components extracted from something, typically by distillation or by solution in alcohol.

Verb:

Convey rapidly and secretly.

Beginning

Invoke the Holy Spirit by praying together:

Come, Holy Spirit, come.
Come as the fire and burn.
Come as the wind and cleanse.
Come as the light and reveal.
Convict, Convert, Consecrate, until we are wholly yours.

Proverbs 20:27

The human spirit is the lamp of the Lord,
    searching every inmost part.

Matthew 3:11

"I baptize you with water for repentance, but one who is more powerful than I is coming after me; I am not worthy to carry his sandals. He will baptize you with the Holy Spirit and fire."

Matthew 3:16

And when Jesus had been baptized, just as he came up from the water, suddenly the heavens were opened to him and he saw the Spirit of God descending like a dove and alighting on him.

Luke 1:35

The angel said to her, "The Holy Spirit will come upon you, and the power of the Most High will overshadow you; therefore the child to be born will be holy; he will be called Son of God."

Luke 3:16

John answered all of them by saying, "I baptize you with water; but one who is more powerful than I is coming; I am not worthy to untie the thong of his sandals. He will baptize you with the Holy Spirit and fire."

John 20:22-23

When he had said this, he breathed on them and said to them, "Receive the Holy Spirit. If you forgive the sins of any, they are forgiven them; if you retain the sins of any, they are retained."

Romans 14:17

For the kingdom of God is not food and drink but righteousness and peace and joy in the Holy Spirit.

ooo

Keep close to Nature's heart . . . and break clear away, once in awhile, and climb a mountain or spend a week in the woods. Wash your spirit clean.

—MUIR, QUOTED BY SAMUEL HALL YOUNG IN *ALASKA DAYS WITH JOHN MUIR* (1915), CHAPTER 7

The world is certainly thought of as a place of spiritual trial, but it is also the confluence of soul and body, word and flesh, where thoughts must become deeds, where goodness must be enacted. This is the great meeting place, the narrow passage where spirit and flesh, word and world, pass into each other. The Bible's aim, as I read it, is not the freeing of the spirit from the world. It is the handbook of their interaction. It says that they cannot be divided; that their mutuality, their unity, is inescapable; that they are not reconciled in division, but in harmony.

—WENDELL BERRY,
*THE ART OF THE COMMONPLACE:
THE AGRARIAN ESSAYS*,
AUGUST 5, 2003

I remind people that there is no Islamic, Christian, or Jewish way of breathing. There is no rich or poor way of breathing. The playing field is utterly leveled. The air of the earth is one and the same air, and this divine wind "blows where it will" (John 3:8)—which appears to be everywhere. No one and no religion can control this spirit. When considered in this way, God is suddenly as available and accessible as the very thing we all do constantly—breathe. Exactly as some teachers of prayer always said, "Stay with the breath, attend to your breath": the same breath that was breathed into Adam's nostrils by this Yahweh (Genesis 2:7); the very breath that Jesus handed over with trust on the cross (John 19:30) and then breathed on us as shalom, forgiveness, and the Holy Spirit all at once (John 20:21–23). And isn't it wonderful

that breath, wind, spirit and air are precisely nothing—
and yet everything?

—FR. RICHARD ROHR, *THE NAKED NOW*

Based on the feminine translation of *spirit*—רוּחַ, *ruach* in
Hebrew and *rucah* in Aramaic, meaning breath, wind,
spirit—and the Greek μήτηρ or *mḗtēr*, which means
mother, we are free to live into the Holy Spirit as fully
feminine. On Pentecost, the fiftieth day after Easter, we
see the symbols of the Holy Spirit—the flames, the wind,
the breath of God, a dove, the color red—all mystery and
confusion and excitement.

> Which of these symbols speaks to the Holy Spirit
> within you?
>
> How might we regard these symbols as particularly
> feminine?

Find your red crayons, your red markers, and draw your Spirit.

> What does She look like?
>
> What does She mean to you?
>
> How do you carry Her into the world?

Ending

Breath Prayer

The breath prayer is a very short prayer of praise and petition. Those who use it feel that it can become as natural as breathing. Just as breathing goes on naturally in the body, prayer can go on naturally in our being . . . Perhaps the best known breath prayer is called the Jesus Prayer: "Lord Jesus Christ, Son of God, have mercy on me a sinner." This prayer had its origin within the Christian tradition of the East and can be traced back to the sixth century . . . This brief prayer seemed to gather and compress within it all one needed to believe in order to be saved.

—RON DELBENE WITH MARY AND HERB MONTGOMERY, *THE HUNGER OF THE HEART: A CALL TO SPIRITUAL GROWTH*

Breath prayers are beautiful and powerful in their two-part simplicity. We breathe in, invoking God's name, and breathe out our request or need from God. The first step to this prayer practice is to listen for the prayer that has profound meaning for you—one that you can repeat so often, it will become as much a part of you as your breath. How will you name God? What is your deepest desire, petition?

To pray The Jesus Prayer:

> Inhale, *Lord Jesus Christ, Son of God*, exhale, *have mercy on me a sinner.*

Shorter version:

> Inhale, *Jesus*, exhale, *have mercy on me.*

Other possibilities, among the many that may speak to you:

> Inhale *Holy One*, exhale *heal me.*
> Inhale *O Lord*, exhale *show me Your way.*
> Inhale *Living God*, exhale *cleanse my spirit.*
> Inhale *Light*, exhale *darkness.*

Practice your breath prayer over and over—while you are driving, walking the dogs, on hold with the insurance company, stirring your spaghetti sauce, getting your teeth cleaned, nursing your baby, watching a PowerPoint presentation, potting chrysanthemums, figuring out fifth grade math, looking at the black of your room in the middle of the night. Pray, pray without ceasing.

God has given to the earth the breath that feeds it. God's breath vibrates in yours, in your voice. It is the breath of God that you breathe.

—THEOPHILUS OF ANTIOCH

Wonder

Definitions

Noun:

A feeling of amazement and admiration, caused by something beautiful, remarkable, or unfamiliar.

'*he observed the intricacy of the ironwork with the wonder of a child*'

A thing or a quality of something that causes wonder.

A person or thing regarded as very good, remarkable, or effective.

Having remarkable properties or abilities.

Desire to know something; feel curious.

Used to express a polite question or request.

Verb:

Feel doubt.

Feel admiration and amazement; marvel.

Beginning

For us to recapture an acute sense of wonder, so unbounded in childhood, we adults must begin in silence and awareness. This meditation exercise is developed from the quatrain beginning "This moment this love comes to rest in me" in *The Essential Rumi*. Spend five minutes breathing in and out the wonder of the world.

> Breathing in: *O let me sense* . . .
> Breathing out: *the world anew.*

When we are stunned to the place beyond words, we're finally starting to get somewhere. It is so much more comfortable to think that we know what it all means, what to expect and how it all hangs together. When we are stunned to the place beyond words, when an aspect of life takes us away from being able to chip away at something until it's down to a manageable size and then to file it nicely away, when all we can say in response is "Wow," that's a prayer.

—ANNE LAMOTT, *HELP, THANKS, WOW*

I think us here to wonder, myself. To wonder. To ask. And that in wondering bout the big things and asking bout the big things, you learn about the little ones, almost by accident. But you never know nothing more about the big things than you start out with. The more I wonder, the more I love.

—ALICE WALKER, *THE COLOR PURPLE*

To Practice This Thought: Become more experienced in the art of "gasping."

—BARBARA KINGSOLVER, *HIGH TIDE IN TUSCON*

O, wonder!
How many goodly creatures are there here!
How beauteous mankind is! O brave new world,
That has such people in't!

—WILLIAM SHAKESPEARE, *THE TEMPEST*

I join my hands in thanks
for the many wonders of life;
for having twenty-four brand-new hours before me.

—THICH NHAT HANH (VIETNAMESE BUDDHIST MONK),
IN *CALL ME BY MY TRUE NAMES*

To practice wondering, illuminate your senses:

> Experiment with various scents to see what memories
> you associate with them. Vanilla, roses, cinnamon,
> coffee, peonies, detergent, mothballs, pine, nutmeg
> are a few suggestions. In your journal or on a piece
> of paper, describe in detail what these smells evoke
> for you.
>
> Listen to different types of music and describe what
> you are hearing. As Ben Ratliff writes in his book
> *Every Song Ever: Twenty Ways to Listen in an Age of
> Musical Plenty*[1] "sounds are running ahead of our
> vocabularies for describing them." What emotions do
> you hear in different types of music? How can music
> change us?
>
> Try a food you have always sworn you do not
> like. Are there new ways to experience this food?
> If not, describe its disgustingness. Eat a straw-
> berry, chocolate, popcorn, an olive, a fig, an apple.
> Describe in detail the sensation of chewing each of
> these foods.
>
> Dr. David Linden in his book *Touch: The Science
> of Hand, Heart, and Mind* (New York: Penguin

---

1. Ben Ratliff, *Every Song Ever: Twenty Ways to Listen in an Age of Musical Plenty* (New York: Farrar, Straus and Giroux, 2016), 7.

Books, 2015) explains that sense of touch deterio-
rates as we age. He claims we may actually avoid falls
by walking barefoot, at least occasionally. Take
off your shoes and walk barefoot on concrete,
grass, sand, dirt. Describe the ground underneath
you.

Look at a painting you have never before seen.
Describe what you see. What emotions do you experience as you describe color, line, composition?

Take an inventory of your awareness of each of your senses:

Which is most dominant? Which is overlooked?

What do we gain from pushing ourselves in our
awareness of wonder?

How might we become more enlightened Christians
in this way?

What aspects of the worship in your religious tradition elicit your wonder?

Reflecting on the Rumi meditation, *This moment
this love comes to rest in me*, how are love and wonder
resting in you?

Ending

Open my eyes,
O God,
to the marvels that surround me.
Show me the wonder
of each breath I take,
of my every
thought,
word
and movement.

—Rebbe Nachman of Breslov,
in *The Gentle Weapon: Prayers for Everyday
and Not-So-Everyday Moments*

Pickling

A few years ago, a group of parishioners gave my husband, Mark, and me several Ball jars full of a mix of pickled sliced hot dogs, onions, and green beans, all swimming around together in pickle juice. I love most pickled things, but I am not a meat-eater, and the hot dogs looked like pathology specimens floating in formalin. I could hardly look at them, much less consider eating them. I dumped that kind gift, all that hard work, in the trash, without even recycling the jars. Now I wish I had just one jar of that gift back. One jar to remind me of all my fermentation, all the onions, beans, even hot dogs, of myself and my life. The slang meaning of the word *pickled* means drunk. I am not drunk, but I am finally coming to grips with my vinegary, briney, floating, sugary pickleness.

The craft of pickling is old, old as the hills. The word *pickle* comes from the Dutch *pekel* or northern

German *pókel*, meaning "salt" or "brine," essential elements of the pickling process. According to the New York Food Museum, archaeologists date the first pickles, of course, to the Mesopotamians in 2400 BC. Cleopatra ate pickles to keep her healthy and beautiful, and Napoleon offered 12,000 francs to the person who could develop the best way to pickle and preserve food for his troops (*http:// www.history.com/news/hungry-history/pickles-throughout -history-2*). Pickling is crucial to the cuisine of many countries—chutneys in India, kimchi in Korea, miso pickles in Japan, pickled herring in Scandinavia, corned beef in Ireland.

Mark F. Sohn, in one of my favorite books, *Appalachian Home Cooking: History, Culture, and Recipes,* writes that at the beginning of the twentieth century, Appalachian folks—who lived without refrigeration—preserved food by pickling, either preserving in a brine (salt or salty water) or an acid like vinegar or lemon juice. They pickled like crazy: cucumbers, beets, corn relish, beans, cabbage, chow chow, watermelon rinds, corn, eggs, grapes, onions, pears, and pigs' feet. Just reading that list, except for the pigs' feet, activates those salivary glands under my ears.

Nothing extra to waste, not the feet of a pig or the rind of the watermelon that most of us pitch aside. As much food as possible was and still is preserved in jar after jar to sustain families throughout the winter.

I always felt torn about my hometown, which was not *in* the Smoky Mountains but at their feet, defined by them. The Cherokees called the Smokies *shaconage* or "place of the blue smoke," for the blue mist that hovers around the peaks and valleys. Reflecting its hardworking blue-collar culture and a history of Appalachian ancestors, our town had neither money nor time to be sophisticated or quaint in the way of some Southern towns. There were beliefs not written anywhere, but well communicated: *Don't get too much education. Don't get too big for your britches. There is only One Way to salvation, so you best get busy.* My parents both left town for college and when they returned—married and then becoming parents of my brother and me—they insisted on teaching us an alternative narrative about education, politics, and faith. I am grateful to Mom and Dad, but boy, did my brother and I feel like weirdos. As difficult and small as my East Tennessee hometown could be, though, it was still my home and I couldn't just throw every experience, every memory, in the trash.

As a child, I spent as much time as possible with my beloved maternal grandmother, Maw, who lived on Morningside Drive. While Mom was reading about food trends and health, buying Roman Meal Bread (when all my friends were still eating the white kind), and baking chicken thighs with brown rice, Maw was still cooking in the Appalachian tradition. I knew Maw's way was how food was supposed to be. She fried bologna in margarine in an iron skillet, cooked her green beans in bacon or pork, all day long. She made tomato aspic with a can of Campbell's Tomato Soup, some Lemon Jell-O, chopped celery, and sliced olives. Mom and I still consider aspic a lovely salad. We drank "Co-Cola" when times were tough. Our only green vegetables, other than green bean casserole with Campbell's Cream of Mushroom Soup and French's Fried Onions at Thanksgiving and Christmas, were bread-and-butter pickles and pickled okra. I still serve this green bean casserole and all the pickles at both holiday celebrations in my own family.

When I moved away, went to college, and got married, I knew better than to eat tacky, unhealthy Southern mountain food. I was sophisticated now, cooking Chicken Marbella from *The Silver Palate Cookbook*, with a whole cup of wine, *capers*, for cryin' out loud, prunes and olives, not to mention a cup of brown sugar. I started reading about cholesterol, bought the *American Heart Association Cookbook*, and made a cheap version of Cioppino, with only fish, chicken broth, and tomatoes. No expensive shrimp, clams, or mussels. Beautiful food, by candlelight, for Mark and me.

I worked hard to lose myself in the blue smoke of sophistication, listening to Sade's *Diamond Life*, while making mushroom spaghetti, so I could be something different, better. It wasn't just that I had grown up in a small town. I had grown up in a town that was not cute, or particularly friendly, one I wanted to love, but just couldn't. I was educated now, maybe too big for my britches. At the same time, my hometown's lack of snobbery, its work ethic, my grandmother's food were part of me. It is not strange for young adults to struggle with identity, but this dissonance was something I carried with me way past young adulthood. I wanted to see myself and wanted others to see my sophisticated side, without the hot dogs. I did not understand that authenticity as one of God's children is within the dissonance, the vinegar. I wanted to jam God, and myself, into a glass jar and seal it with boiling water.

Mark, our three daughters, and I lived in sophisticated cities and small towns before we wound up in Southwest Virginia, in the Blue Ridge Mountains. The girls and I love to cook and we all know how to order well in different kinds of restaurants, both high and low. It's simple: *try everything*. Every city, every town has defining foods that provide insight into the way people live, what they believe, who they are. Chicago's deep-dish pizza and hot dogs, North Carolina's barbeque and cornbread, South Carolina's shrimp and grits and peaches, Louisville's Derby Pie and Henry Bain sauce. Melting pots all over the place. The only way to do it is to pick up your fork and go in without fear or shame. There will be gristle, but you can spit that

out. There will be anchovies and they are salty and deli-
cious. You will have barbeque sauce on your lips and your
white shirt, but it will come clean.

Our family loves to poke fun at each other, as long
as it's kind. I am the ringleader. It might be a universal
experience or maybe the redneck in me, but the minute
somebody else outside the circle starts making fun of my
family or the people I love, I become crazy defensive and
protective. After I lived away for so many years, I have
become the same way about the Appalachian Mountains.
My brother and I can joke all we want about Tennessee,
but as soon as a Midwesterner joins in, I have a speech:
*Don't judge people you don't understand. Rest assured there
are good and bad within all of us, dude. Have you ever had a
real biscuit or green bean casserole?* Sometimes I practice the
speech on myself. The defensiveness has taught me not to
throw away the good gifts, to realize what's inside, though
not perfect, is a part of it all.

Pickles become what they are with helpful bacteria.
Salt, or vinegar, crowd out the rotting microbes, which
produce the lactic acid, or acetic acid, that sustains a good
long life. Within that jar is the hard work of someone's
hands. Growing, picking, washing, slicing the cucumbers.
Buying, measuring, mixing salt, vinegar, sugar, spices.
Waiting, waiting for the long, cold winter while doing all
the other work, endless other chores, taking care of other

people. Honor those good gifts. Within that jar is a wild mixture of humanity—hot dogs, green beans, and onions. You might not eat meat, but it is all suspended together in the pickle juice, for better and for worse. It's just the mix.

Abundance

Definitions

Noun:

A very large quantity of something.

The state or condition of having a copious quantity of something; plentifulness.

Plentifulness of the good things of life; prosperity.

The quantity or amount of something present in a particular area, volume, or sample.

Origin:

Middle English: from Latin *abundantia*, from abundant—'overflowing,' from the verb *abundare*.

Beginning

What abundances have, or have not, been present in your life this week?

What are words, thoughts, emotions you associate with *abundance*?

What are the differences between a worldview of abundance and one of scarcity?

How might a spiritual vision of abundance differ from a cultural one?

How do we regard a worldview of abundance in the midst of the hunger and poverty faced by so many?

When you have abundant time, read or re-read the book of Exodus. Walter Brueggemann reflects on the events of Exodus:

In answer to the people's fears and complaints, something extraordinary happens. God's love comes trickling down in the form of bread. They say, "Manhue?"—Hebrew for "What is it?"—and the word "manna" is born. They had never before received bread as a free gift that they couldn't control, predict, plan for, or own. The meaning of this strange narrative is that the gifts of life are indeed given by a generous God. It's a wonder, it's a miracle, it's an embarrassment, it's irrational, but God's abundance transcends the market economy.

—"The Liturgy of Abundance, the Myth of Scarcity: Consumerism and Religious Life," *https://www.uucr.org/sites/default/files/sermons /readings/The%20Liturgy%20of%20Abundance %2C%20The%20Myth%20of%20Scarcity.pdf*

What are other stories of abundance from the Bible?

If you can't find a Bible amidst abundant books, laundry, dog hair in your house, reflect on the following psalms. How does the language reveal God's abundance? How can we further expand our definition of spiritual abundance?

Psalm 5:7

But I, through the abundance of your steadfast love,
    will enter your house,
I will bow down towards your holy temple
    in awe of you.

Psalm 69:13

But as for me, my prayer is to you, O Lord.
    At an acceptable time, O God,
    in the abundance of your steadfast love, answer me.
With your faithful help . . .

Psalm 106:45

For their sake he remembered his covenant,
    and showed compassion according to the abundance
    of his steadfast love.

Psalm 104:1–23

Bless the Lord, O my soul.
    O Lord my God, you are very great.
You are clothed with honour and majesty,
    wrapped in light as with a garment.
You stretch out the heavens like a tent,
    you set the beams of your chambers on the waters,
you make the clouds your chariot,
    you ride on the wings of the wind,
you make the winds your messengers,
    fire and flame your ministers.

You set the earth on its foundations,
    so that it shall never be shaken.
You cover it with the deep as with a garment;
    the waters stood above the mountains.
At your rebuke they flee;
    at the sound of your thunder they take to flight.
They rose up to the mountains, ran down to the valleys
    to the place that you appointed for them.
You set a boundary that they may not pass,
    so that they might not again cover the earth.

You make springs gush forth in the valleys;
    they flow between the hills,
giving drink to every wild animal;
    the wild asses quench their thirst.
By the streams the birds of the air have their habitation;
    they sing among the branches.
From your lofty abode you water the mountains;
    the earth is satisfied with the fruit of your work.

You cause the grass to grow for the cattle,
    and plants for people to use,
to bring forth food from the earth,
    and wine to gladden the human heart,
oil to make the face shine,
    and bread to strengthen the human heart.
The trees of the Lord are watered abundantly,
    the cedars of Lebanon that he planted.
In them the birds build their nests;
    the stork has its home in the fir trees.
The high mountains are for the wild goats;
    the rocks are a refuge for the coneys.
You have made the moon to mark the seasons;
    the sun knows its time for setting.

You make darkness, and it is night,
   when all the animals of the forest come creeping out.
The young lions roar for their prey,
   seeking their food from God.
When the sun rises, they withdraw
   and lie down in their dens.
People go out to their work
   and to their labour until the evening.

ooo

Both abundance and lack exist simultaneously in our lives, as parallel realities. It is always our conscious choice which secret garden we will tend . . . when we choose not to focus on what is missing from our lives but are grateful for the abundance that's present—love, health, family, friends, work, the joys of nature and personal pursuits that bring us pleasure—the wasteland of illusion falls away and we experience Heaven on earth.

—SARAH BAN BREATHNACH, AUTHOR OF
SIMPLE ABUNDANCE: A DAYBOOK OF COMFORT

Make peace with the universe. Take joy in it.
It will turn to gold. Resurrection
will be now. Every moment,
a new beauty.
And never any boredom?
Instead this abundant, pouring
noise of many springs in your ears.

—RUMI, *THE ESSESNTIAL RUMI*,

BY JALAL AL-DIN RUMI,

TRANS. BY COLEMAN BARKS, JOHN MOYNE,

2004, HARPERCOLLINS

List the sources of abundance within you.

> Draw two columns. On the left, list all of the areas
> of scarcity in your life, the places where you feel
> shorted. On the right, try to counter each place of
> scarcity with one of abundance. For example, on the
> left, you may write "time" or "sleep." On the right,
> you may list "great dance songs on my Spotify" or
> "love for my children." If you continue to do this
> over time, either on paper or in your mind, you will

start to view the world through the lens of abundance rather than scarcity.

Pop popcorn, scrounge for some Junior Mints, find your person, dog, or cat—whoever will share your blanket—and watch the original Gene Wilder version of *Charlie and the Chocolate Factory*. How do different views of scarcity and abundance affect the characters in the movie?

Share abundantly whatever is abundant within you—kindness, love, laughter, art, money, compassion, wisdom, books, food, jokes, hope, compliments, justice, flowers, words, touch, coffee, insight, chocolate, tears, passion, music, prayer, poetry, light.

Ending

Praise Song

by Barbara Crooker

Praise the light of late November,
the thin sunlight that goes deep in the bones.
Praise the crows chattering in the oak trees;

though they are clothed in night, they do not
despair. Praise what little there's left:
the small boats of milkweed pods, husks, hulls,
shells, the architecture of trees. Praise the meadow
of dried weeds: yarrow, goldenrod, chicory,
the remains of summer. Praise the blue sky
that hasn't cracked yet. Praise the sun slipping down
behind the beechnuts, praise the quilt of leaves
that covers the grass: Scarlet Oak, Sweet Gum,
Sugar Maple. Though darkness gathers, praise our crazy
fallen world; it's all we have, and it's never enough.[1]

---

1. Barbara Crooker, *Radiance* (Cincinnati: Word Press, 2005), 82. Used by permission.

Change

Definitions

Verb:

Make or become different.

Move from one to another.

Give up or get rid of (something) in exchange for something else.

Remove (something dirty or faulty) and replace it with another of the same kind.

Noun:

An act or process through which something becomes different.

The substitution of one thing for another.

An alteration or modification.

A new or refreshingly different experience.

A clean garment or garments as a replacement for something one is wearing.

Menopause.

The moon's arrival at a fresh phase, typically at the new moon.

Coins as opposed to banknotes.

Money given in exchange for the same sum in larger units.

Money returned to someone as the balance of the sum paid for something.

An order in which a peal of bells can be rung (usually *changes*).

Historical:

A place where merchants met to do business.

Beginning

Words—along with habits, thoughts, and beliefs—can become stagnant over time if they are never awakened by newness. The word *change*, with myriad definitions, holds great literal and metaphorical possibility. How might the many definitions of *change* inspire us to see *change itself* in a new light?

What are words associated with change that come to your mind?

How is change a reality, or not, in your life right now?

In a Christian context, the many changes of our lives occur in relationship with God. It is important to remember we are not alone.

Genesis 18:9-15

They said to him, "Where is your wife Sarah?" And he said, "There, in the tent." Then one said, "I will surely return to you in due season, and your wife Sarah shall have a son." And Sarah was listening at the tent entrance behind him. Now Abraham and Sarah were old, advanced in age; it had ceased to be with Sarah after the manner of women. So Sarah laughed to herself, saying, "After I have grown old, and my husband is old, shall I have pleasure?" The Lord said to Abraham, "Why did Sarah laugh, and say, 'Shall I indeed bear a child, now that I am old?' Is anything too wonderful for the Lord? At the set time I will return to you, in due season, and Sarah shall have a son." But Sarah denied, saying, "I did not laugh"; for she was afraid. He said, "Oh yes, you did laugh."

What is the meaning of this *change* story?

What are the other significant *change* stories of the Bible that hold meaning for you? Why?

Matthew 18:3

". . . Truly I tell you, unless you change and become like children, you will never enter the kingdom of heaven."

ooo

Yesterday I was clever, so I wanted to change the world. Today I am wise, so I am changing myself.

—RUMI

Plus ça change, plus c'est la même chose. [The more it changes, the more it's the same thing.]

—JEAN BAPTISTE ALPHONSE KARR
(1808–1890), FRENCH CRITIC AND NOVELIST,
LES GUÊPES, JANUARY 1849

Some changes look negative on the surface but you will soon realize that space is being created in your life for something new to emerge.

—ECKHART TOLLE, A NEW EARTH: AWAKENING
TO YOUR LIFE'S PURPOSE

Questions for consideration:

> What have been the major changes of your life?
>
> What were the emotions that surrounded those changes?
>
> In what ways did you feel God's presence or absence in the midst of those changes?
>
> What have you found most helpful to you in dealing with change?
>
> Who are the people/what are the experiences in your life that have helped you most change?

Ending

The Serenity Prayer

God, grant me the Serenity
To accept the things I cannot change . . .
Courage to change the things I can,
And Wisdom to know the difference.
Living one day at a time,
Enjoying one moment at a time,

Accepting hardship as the pathway to peace.
Taking, as He did, this sinful world as it is,
Not as I would have it.
Trusting that He will make all things right
if I surrender to His will.
That I may be reasonably happy in this life,
And supremely happy with Him forever in the next.
Amen.

—Reinhold Niebuhr (1892–1971)

Red

Definitions

Adjective:

Of a color at the end of the spectrum next to orange and opposite violet, as of blood, fire, or rubies.

(Of a person or their face) flushed or rosy, especially with embarrassment, anger, or heat.

(Of a person's eyes) bloodshot or having pink rims, especially with tiredness or crying.

(Of hair or fur) of a reddish-brown or orange-brown color.

Of or denoting the suits hearts and diamonds in a pack of cards.

(Of wine) made from dark grapes and colored by their skins.

Denoting a red light or flag used as a signal to stop.

Used to denote something forbidden, dangerous, or urgent.

(Of a ski run) of the second-highest level of difficulty, as indicated by red markers positioned along it.

Physics:

Denoting one of three colors of quark.

Involving bloodshed or violence.

South African:

(Of a Xhosa) coming from a traditional tribal culture.

Noun:

Red color or pigment.

Red clothes or material.

A red thing.

A red wine.

A red ball in snooker or billiards.

A red light.

The situation of owing money to a bank or making a loss in a business operation.

Phrases:

red as a beetroot

- (Of a person) red-faced, typically through embarrassment.

red in tooth and claw

- Involving savage or merciless conflict or competition.

the red planet

- A name for Mars.

a red rag to a bull

- An object, utterance, or act that is certain to provoke someone.

Beginning

What are the thoughts, emotions, words that come to mind when you see *red*?

Exodus 12:13

The blood shall be a sign for you on the houses where you live: when I see the blood, I will pass over you, and no plague shall destroy you when I strike the land of Egypt.

The history of the red doors of many Episcopal and Lutheran churches seems to be anecdotal, rather than documented history, but one theory, based on the Exodus passage, suggests that the red doors marked physical and spiritual sanctuary for those within. During the Middle Ages, an enemy could supposedly not pursue his victim across this sacred threshold. Today, many Episcopal and Lutheran churches proclaim with their red doors that the sacred space within is filled with the strength and power of the Holy Spirit, a protective place of refuge and forgiveness.

Isaiah 1:18

Come now, let us argue it out,
    says the Lord:
though your sins are like scarlet,
    they shall be like snow;
though they are red like crimson,
    they shall become like wool.

Matthew 27:28

They stripped him and put a scarlet robe on him . . .

Revelation 17:3

So he carried me away in the spirit into a wilderness, and I saw a woman sitting on a scarlet beast that was full of blasphemous names, and it had seven heads and ten horns.

ooo

Leah had dreamed once of a pomegranate split open to reveal eight red seeds. Zilpah said the dream meant she would have eight healthy children, and my mother knew those words to be true the way she knew how to make bread and beer.

—Anita Diamant, *The Red Tent*

Once upon a time there was a sweet little girl. Everyone who saw her liked her, but most of all her grandmother, who did not know what to give the child next. Once she gave her a little cap made of red velvet. Because it suited her so well, and she wanted to wear it all the time, she came to be known as Little Red Cap.

—Grimm Fairy Tale,
"Little Red Cap"
(Little Red Riding Hood),
Jacob and Wilhelm,
Folk and Fairy Tales

It [the scarlet letter] had the effect of a spell, taking her out of the ordinary relations with humanity, and enclosing her in a sphere by herself.

—Nathaniel Hawthorne, *The Scarlet Letter*

Write about the red caps or the red letters you have worn in your life. Are there ways you feel you have stood out to others, either in a positive or negative way? Did you overcome the experience(s) or accept it/them somehow?

What are the ways we can more easily embrace the red of passion, the red of anger in our lives? What are the fires in our lives we need to either extinguish or sit down beside to warm our hands and souls?

Ending

Imagine yourself like the color red: ablaze with confidence, embers of passion rising up to your heart, through the veins in your strong and capable arms. Take with you its remarkable color, standing out among a world of greys and muted greens. Rise above dullness and emit ruby sparks, like the rising red flames of a forest fire.

Begin to see your world in reds.

A red lipstick smeared on your pout announcing:

Yes I'm here.

Red brick on the grounds you walk, giving you joy in the
clip clop clip clop as you pass by.

Red summer berries sweeter staining your fingertips as
you bite in and relish in their sweetness. The redness
of your cheeks when you watch someone you love
thrive, because you're too old and too wonderful to be
jealous of another one's success.

The red drops from a knife nick reminding you that
you're alive and can feel, and should give up trying to
make zucchini noodles.

Remind yourself that you're warm like red, bursting
with desires and dazzling others with an element
of surprise.

Let yourself be red, as fiery and wild as it may be.

—Sarah M. Bourlakas

(written for this book)

Feast

Definitions

Noun:

A large meal, typically a celebratory one.

A plentiful supply of something enjoyable.

An annual religious celebration.

A day dedicated to a particular saint.

Verb:

Eat and drink sumptuously.

Eat large quantities of.

Beginning

The Hebrew word for *feasts, moadim,* means appointed times. Seven appointed feast days in the Episcopal Church—Easter Day, Ascension Day, Pentecost, Trinity Sunday, All Saints' Day, Christmas Day, Epiphany—reiterate the joyous, abundant inclusivity of the table of Jesus.

What words, emotions come to mind when you consider the word *feast*?

Proverbs 9:5-6

"Come, eat of my bread
  and drink of the wine I have mixed.
⁶ Lay aside immaturity, and live,
  and walk in the way of insight."

Psalm 36:8

They feast on the abundance of your house,
and you give them drink from the river of your delights.

Isaiah 25:6

On this mountain the Lord of hosts will make for
  all peoples
  a feast of rich food, a feast of well-matured wines,

of rich food filled with marrow, of well-matured wines strained clear.

Matthew 22:2

"The kingdom of heaven may be compared to a king who gave a wedding feast for his son."

Luke 14:15–24

The Parable of the Great Dinner

One of the dinner guests, on hearing this, said to him, "Blessed is anyone who will eat bread in the kingdom of God!" Then Jesus said to him, "Someone gave a great dinner and invited many. At the time for the dinner he sent his slave to say to those who had been invited, 'Come; for everything is ready now.' But they all alike began to make excuses. The first said to him, 'I have bought a piece of land, and I must go out and see it; please accept my regrets.' Another said, 'I have bought five yoke of oxen, and I am going to try them out; please accept my regrets.' Another said, 'I have just been married, and therefore I cannot come.' So the slave returned and reported this to his master. Then the owner of the house became angry and said to his slave, 'Go out at once into the streets and lanes of the town and bring in the poor, the crippled, the blind, and the lame.' And the slave said, 'Sir, what you ordered has been done, and there is still room.' Then the master said to the slave, 'Go out into the roads and lanes, and compel people to come in, so that my house may be filled. For I tell you, none of those who were invited will taste my dinner.'"

Luke 24:28–35

The Feast at Emmaus

As they came near the village to which they were going, he walked ahead as if he were going on. But they urged him strongly, saying, "Stay with us, because it is almost evening and the day is now nearly over." So he went in to stay with them. When he was at the table with them, he took bread, blessed and broke it, and gave it to them. Then their eyes were opened, and they recognized him; and he vanished from their sight. They said to each other, "Were not our hearts burning within us while he was talking to us on the road, while he was opening the scriptures to us?" That same hour they got up and returned to Jerusalem; and they found the eleven and their companions gathered together. They were saying, "The Lord has risen indeed, and he has appeared to Simon!" Then they told what had happened on the road, and how he had been made known to them in the breaking of the bread.

All eleven of the Christian meals, found only in Luke's Gospel, reveal the Kingdom of God in miniature: *all* are welcome, *all* are reconciled. Through these meals, Jesus demonstrates, models hospitality and servanthood. When the disciples get to Emmaus, even though they don't recognize Jesus—he is a *stranger* to them—they invite him to stay and eat because it's late. It is not until they share a meal together that the disciples recognize Jesus. *When we share meals, we move from being strangers to knowing each other, knowing God.*

ooo

An intelligently planned feast is like a summing up of the whole world, where each part is represented by its envoys.

—Jean-Anthelme Brillat-Savarin,
The Physiology of Taste, 1825

Be not angry or sour at table; whatever may happen put on the cheerful mien, for good humor makes one dish a feast.

—From a Shaker manual, *Gentle Manners*

If you could have a feast and invite any five people, living or dead, whom would you invite and what foods would you want to serve/eat?

> Watch and discuss *Babette's Feast, http://www.imdb
> .com/title/tt0092603/*, a subtitled Danish film,
> considered by many to be one of the greatest food
> movies of all time. The movie more importantly lays
> beautifully on the table themes of faith, sensuality,
> gratitude, and community.

Ending

Blessings

Loving God, bless all those gathered here today
as we come together in friendship and fellowship.
Thank you for the blessings of our individual
and collective God-given gifts.
Place in our hearts the desire to make a difference
to our families, to our community, to our country,
and to the many cultures and peoples worldwide.
Give us balance in times of distraction and uncertainty.
Help us move towards our goals with determination
and always with an abundant sense of humor.
Thank you for food in a world where many know only
     hunger;

For our faith in a world where many know fear;

For friends in a world where many know only loneliness.

Please bless this food we are about to share, those who
    prepared it, those who serve it,

and those who have worked to make today the special
    occasion that it is.

For all of this we give you thanks.

—Izola White, Jesuit blessing

May the blessing of the five loaves and the two fishes
which God shared out among the five thousand be ours.
May the King who did the sharing bless our sharing and
our co-sharing.

—Irish blessing

Sung Blessings from Kanuga,
https://www.kanuga.org
(and many other camps)

Johnny Appleseed

Oh, the Lord is good to me (clap, clap)
And so I thank the Lord (clap, clap)
For giving me the things I need:
The sun and the rain and the apple seed

The Lord is good to me.

Amen!

Superman

Sung to the *Superman* theme song (Put both arms up in the air and pretend you are flying like Superman.)

Thank you Lord for giving us food.

Thank you Lord for giving us food.

Thank you, Redeemer.

Thank you, Sustainer.

Thank you Lord for giving us food.

Amen (in a deep voice).

from God; for no one can do these signs that you do apart from the presence of God." Jesus answered him, "Very truly, I tell you, no one can see the kingdom of God without being born from above."

ooo

What hath night to do with sleep?

—JOHN MILTON, PARADISE LOST

Night falls. Or has fallen. Why is it that night falls, instead of rising, like the dawn? Yet if you look east, at sunset, you can see night rising, not falling; darkness lifting into the sky, up from the horizon, like a black sun behind cloud cover. Like smoke from an unseen fire, a line of fire just below the horizon, brushfire or a burning city. Maybe night falls because it's heavy, a thick curtain pulled up over the eyes. Wool blanket.

—MARGARET ATWOOD,
THE HANDMAID'S TALE, P. 191

Never shall I forget that night, the first night in camp, which has turned my life into one long night, seven times cursed and seven times sealed. . . .

—ELIE WIESEL, NIGHT, P. 34

In the eighth chapter, titled "Night on the Great Beach," Beston writes: "Our fantastic civilization has fallen out of touch with many aspects of nature, and with none more completely than night. . . . Are modern folk, perhaps, afraid of the night? Do they fear that vast serenity, the mystery of infinite space, the austerity of the stars? Having made themselves at home in a civilization obsessed with power, which explains its whole world in terms of energy, do they fear at night for their dull acquiescence and the pattern of their beliefs? Be the answer what it will, today's civilization is full of people who have not the slightest notion of the character or the poetry of night, who have never even seen night. Yet to live thus, to know only artificial night, is as absurd and evil as to know only artificial day. . . . Night is very beautiful on this great beach. It is the true other half of the day's tremendous wheel; no lights without meaning stab or trouble it; it is beauty, it is fulfillment, it is rest."

—MARIA POPOVA, DISCUSSING *IN PRAISE OF DARKNESS: HENRY BESTON ON HOW THE BEAUTY OF NIGHT NOURISHES THE HUMAN SPIRIT*, ON HER BLOG, BRAIN PICKINGS, JUNE 4, 2015, *HTTPS://WWW.BRAINPICKINGS.ORG /2015/06/04/HENRY-BESTON-NIGHT-OUTERMOST-HOUSE/*

The night is full of terrors, from witches to loneliness, yet it is a labyrinth of mystery and beauty. The strangest and most marvellous art experience I have had this year involved going into total darkness equipped only with a torch. After clambering over slippery, sharp surfaces and through narrow, claustrophobic apertures, we finally reached a pitch-black gallery where spotlights were turned on to reveal the art. This was not an installation at Tate Modern but a cave in the Pyrenees. Here, deep underground, ice age artists drew bison and ibex with charcoal 13,000 years ago. Why did the ice age artists explore such deep, dark places? Why is the oldest art in the world shrouded in permanent night? It has to be that our imaginations crave darkness. Only in the dark can we forget the banal distraction of daylit reality and enter a visionary realm of dreams. Art is a creature of the night.

—JONATHAN JONES, "THE GUARDIAN," *DARK ARTS: HOW NIGHT INSPIRES GREAT PAINTERS*, SEPTEMBER 27, 2016

Are there times when night has brought you creativity or clarity?

Spend time with, study, experience, gaze at a night painting, such as Geertgen tot Sint Jans's *The Nativity at Night* (1490), Vincent Van Gogh's *Café Terrace at Night* (1888) or *The Starry Night* (1889), or Edward Hopper's *Nighthawks* (1942).

On a lovely piece of paper, write what you see. What is the life of the night depicted? How do the color choices affect you? What is the rhythm of the work? What effects does the work have on your emotion, your intellect, your spirit? What is the universality of the painting?

Ending

New Zealand Prayer for Night

Lord,
it is night.
The night is for stillness.
Let us be still in the presence of God.
It is night after a long day.
What has been done has been done;
what has not been done has not been done;
let it be.
The night is dark.
Let our fears of the darkness of the world and of our
    own lives
rest in you.
The night is quiet.

Let the quietness of your peace enfold us,
all dear to us,
and all who have no peace.
The night heralds the dawn.
Let us look expectantly to a new day,
new joys,
new possibilities.
In your name we pray.
Amen.[1]

1. "Lord It Is Night . . . ," *A New Zealand Prayer Book—He Karakia Mihinare o Aotearoa* (San Francisco: HarperSanFrancisco, 1997), 184. Used by permission.

Laugh

Definitions

Verb:

Make the spontaneous sounds and movements of the face and body that are the instinctive expressions of lively amusement and sometimes also of derision.

Laugh at—Treat with ridicule or scorn.

Laugh something off—Dismiss something by treating it in a light-hearted way.

Be in a fortunate or successful position.

Noun:

Something that causes laughter; a source of fun, amusement, or derision.

A person who is good fun or amusing company.

Phrases:

laugh all the way to the bank

have the last laugh

he who laughs last laughs longest

laugh one's head off

laugh in someone's face

the laugh is on me (or you, him, etc.)

a laugh a minute

laugh oneself silly (or sick)

no laughing matter

Beginning

What words, thoughts come to mind when you consider *laugh, laughing, laughter*?

Genesis 17:17

Then Abraham fell on his face and laughed, and said to himself, "Can a child be born to a man who is a hundred years old? Can Sarah, who is ninety years old, bear a child?"

Genesis 18:12–13, 15

So Sarah laughed to herself, saying, "After I have grown old, and my husband is old, shall I have pleasure?" The Lord said to Abraham, "Why did Sarah laugh, and say, 'Shall I indeed bear a child, now that I am old?'" . . . But Sarah denied, saying, "I did not laugh"; for she was afraid. He said, "Oh yes, you did laugh."

Job 8:21

He will yet fill your mouth with laughter,
   and your lips with shouts of joy.

Psalm 126:2

Then our mouth was filled with laughter,
   and our tongue with shouts of joy;
then it was said among the nations,
   "The Lord has done great things for them."

ooo

Laughter is the closest thing to the grace of God.

—KARL BARTH, THEOLOGIAN

Power, Money, Persuasion, Supplication, Persecution—
these can lift a colossal humbug—push it a little—crowd
it a little—weaken it a little, century by century: but only
Laughter can blow it to rags and atoms at a blast. Against
the assault of Laughter nothing can stand.

—MARK TWAIN, "THE CHRONICLE OF YOUNG
SATAN," *MYSTERIOUS STRANGER MANUSCRIPTS*

There is a thin line that separates laughter and pain, com-
edy and tragedy, humor and hurt.

—ERMA BOMBECK, *GOODREADS.COM*

Laughter is carbonated holiness.

—ANNE LAMOTT, *PLAN B: FURTHER THOUGHTS ON FAITH*

Humour is, in fact, a prelude to faith; and laughter is the
beginning of prayer.

—REINHOLD NIEBUHR, *THE ESSENTIAL REINHOLD
NIEBUHR: SELECTED ESSAYS AND ADDRESSES*

We are perhaps permitted tragedy as a sort of merciful com-
edy: because the frantic energy of divine things would knock
us down like a drunken farce. We can take our own tears
more lightly than we could take the tremendous levities of
the angels. So we sit perhaps in a starry chamber of silence,
while the laughter of the heavens is too loud for us to hear.

—G.K. CHESTERTON, *ORTHODOXY*

My fellow researchers and I found that while both sexes laugh a lot, females laugh more. In cross-gender conversations, females laughed 126% more than their male counterparts, meaning that women tend to do the most laughing while males tend to do the most laugh-getting.

—ROBERT PROVINE, "THE SCIENCE OF LAUGHTER,"
PSYCHOLOGY TODAY (ONLINE)

Although we may know instinctively that laughter benefits our well-being, the Mayo Clinic has data to back up our experience. Laughter induces actual physical changes in our bodies and brains by:

Stimulating organs such as the heart and lungs

Activating and relieving the stress response

Soothing tension by stimulating circulation and aiding muscle relaxation

Improving the immune system by releasing neuropeptides

Relieving pain by causing the body to produce natural painkillers

—MAYO CLINIC ONLINE, "STRESS MANAGEMENT,"
HTTP://WWW.MAYOCLINIC.ORG/HEALTHY-LIFESTYLE
/STRESS-MANAGEMENT/IN-DEPTH/STRESS-RELIEF/ART-20044456

> What are ways laughter has brought you together with someone?
>
> What are your greatest memories of laughter?
>
> Who are the people, what are the books, movies, TV shows that make you laugh and why?

Laughter is such a personal, natural experience that we can neither teach it nor force it to occur. We can, however, practice laughter so we reap the emotional and physical benefits as much as possible. As a group, play the game of Things. Although this game is available to buy, *https://www.thegameofthings.com,* it is simple to play with slips of paper and pens/pencils. Things can be played with varying group sizes and the only objective of the game is LAUGHTER.

Everyone needs a stack of small slips of paper and a pen or a pencil (maybe reading glasses). The group needs two baskets or boxes—one for things and one for responses.

1. Players begin by writing five or so (depending on time and group size) topics or *things*. Here are some suggestions, but be creative in thinking of your own topics (and please let me know your best ones):

   Things a doctor shouldn't do while performing surgery

   Things about people that frustrate you

Things big dogs think when they see a Chihuahua

Things cats think about humans

Things children shouldn't know

Things not to tell your mother

Things people do when no one is looking

Things that are better late than never

Things that confirm your small town is backward

Things that happen once in a blue moon

Things that should come with a manual

Things that should not be lumpy

Things you could use as an excuse on Judgment Day

Things you return from your Christmas gifts

Things you shouldn't use as an opening line

Things your parents forgot to tell you

2. Fold all of the *things*, put them in a basket, then select a reader. Without looking, the reader draws one slip from the basket and reads the topic out loud.

3. All players, including the reader, write a response to the topic on one of their pieces of paper, fold the response up tight, then put it into the response basket.

4. The reader then reads all the responses aloud twice. The player to the left of the reader tries to match each

response to a player. You don't have to know every-body to laugh and try to match the responses. Let everyone have a chance to be the reader. The official rules suggest keeping score for correct answers, but why bother?

Ending

Prayer for Laughter

God of grace, God of love and laughter, we thank you that we are so wondrously created and that we are made for relationship with you and with one another. We thank you for laughter with friends and loved ones. We thank you for the laughter of children, and the song it creates in our hearts.

By your great unending love, you inspire in us a spirit of imagination and creativity. Help us to use that spirit to play more, to laugh more, and to create beauty in every way possible. Remind us to laugh out loud, for doing so will heal some of the wounds within us. Not all, but some.

God, we pray for those who cannot find their laughter today. For those who are grieving, or suffering illness of body, mind or spirit . . . for those who are lonely and in need of someone to share their time and friendship.

May these and the troubles of all your people be soothed, blessed, and comforted by your holy presence. May we each find the laughter within us that sets our spirits free, and in that freedom, may we take your love into every part of our lives.[1]

---

1. The Rev. Sue Ivany, RevGalPals, Thunder Bay, Ontario, Canada, United Church of Canada (Ordained Ministry Personnel), March 30, 2008.

Beauty

Definitions

Noun:

A combination of qualities, such as shape, color, or form, that pleases the aesthetic senses, especially the sight.

A combination of qualities that pleases the intellect.

Beginning

What are words and emotions that come to mind when you think of the word *beauty*?

Psalm 50:2

Out of Zion, the perfection of beauty,
    God shines forth.

ooo

Nothing is so beautiful as Spring—
When weeds, in wheels, shoot long and lovely and lush;
Thrush's eggs look little low heavens, and thrush
Through the echoing timber does so rinse and wring
The ear, it strikes like lightnings to hear him sing;
The glassy peartree leaves and blooms, they brush
The descending blue; that blue is all in a rush
With richness; the racing lambs too have fair their fling.

—"Spring," Gerard Manley Hopkins

For beauty is nothing but the beginning of terror which we are barely able to endure, and it amazes us so, because it serenely disdains to destroy us. Every angel is terrible.

—Rainer Maria Rilke, *Duino Elegies*

Here is the world. Beautiful and terrible things will happen. Don't be afraid.

—Frederick Buechner, *Beyond Words: Daily Readings in the ABC's of Faith*

Using the questions below, discuss the ways beauty is associated with "terrible" in the two quotations that follow.

How is the Cross an example of the coexistence of beauty and terror?

How might this association affect or change our perception of beauty in the world?

Are there ways to find beauty amidst horror in our world? How so?

Dwell on the beauty of life. Watch the stars, and see yourself running with them.

—Marcus Aurelius, *Meditations*

I don't think of all the misery, but of the beauty that still remains.

—Anne Frank, *The Diary of a Young Girl*

The most beautiful people we have known are those who have known defeat, known suffering, known struggle, known loss, and have found their way out of the depths. These persons have an appreciation, a sensitivity, and an understanding of life that fills them with compassion, gentleness, and a deep loving concern. Beautiful people do not just happen.

—Elisabeth Kübler-Ross, *Death: The Final Stage of Growth*

You're just as pretty as she is. Prettier.

—Mom

Watch the Dove Real Beauty Sketches, *https://www.youtube
.com/watch?v=litXW91UauE.*

> *Disclaimer: Dove is a corporation in the business of mak-
> ing money from selling beauty products. This video has
> been criticized and parodied, perhaps with good reason.
> However, these human stories spark interesting conversa-
> tion about what beauty is and how we do and do not per-
> ceive ourselves as God's beautiful beings.*

The practice of seeing ourselves as beautiful is an
important step in seeing beauty beyond ourselves, in
others.

> What informs your ideas about what true beauty is?
>
> Seeing yourself as a child of God, how would you
> describe your own beauty?

Ending

Worship the Lord in the beauty of holiness; let the whole earth tremble before him.

—Evening Prayer, BCP, Psalm 96:9

We give you thanks, most gracious God,

for the beauty of earth and sky and sea;

for the richness of mountains, plains, and rivers;

for the songs of birds and the loveliness of flowers.

We praise you for these good gifts,

and pray that we may safeguard them for our posterity.

Grant that we may continue to grow in our grateful

    enjoyment of your abundant creation,

to the honor and glory of your Name, now and forever.

    Amen.

—Thanksgivings for the Natural Order, BCP

Movement

Definitions

Noun:

An act of moving.

An arrival or departure of an aircraft.

The activities and whereabouts of someone during a particular period of time.

General activity or bustle.

The moving parts of a mechanism, especially a clock or watch.

Change or development.

A group of people working together to advance their shared political, social, or artistic ideas.

A campaign undertaken by a political, social, or artistic movement.

Music:

A principal division of a longer musical work, self-sufficient in terms of key, tempo, and structure.

Beginning

How do your body and mind react when you hear the word *move* or *movement*?

Genesis 1:21

So God created the great sea monsters and every living creature that moves, of every kind, with which the waters swarm, and every winged bird of every kind. And God saw that it was good.

Psalm 16:8

I keep the Lord always before me;

because he is at my right hand, I shall not be moved.

Matthew 17:20

He said to them, "Because of your little faith. For truly I tell you, if you have faith the size of a mustard seed, you will say to this mountain, 'Move from here to there,' and it will move; and nothing will be impossible for you."

Luke 14:10

"But when you are invited, go and sit down at the lowest place, so that when your host comes, he may say to you, 'Friend, move up higher'; then you will be honoured in the presence of all who sit at the table with you."

ooo

All that is important is this one moment in movement. Make the moment important, vital, and worth living. Do not let it slip away unnoticed and unused.

—MARTHA GRAHAM (1884–1991), AMERICAN MODERN DANCER AND CHOREOGRAPHER

I move, therefore I am.

—HARUKI MURAKAMI, *1Q85*

To me, if life boils down to one thing, it's movement. To live is to keep moving.

—JERRY SEINFELD

Will you, won't you, will you, won't you, will you join the dance?

—Lewis Carroll, *Alice's Adventures in Wonderland*,
Chapter X: The Lobster Quadrille

Practice mindful movement:

There are many possibilities for a short movement exercise, preferably one that combines body, mind, and spirit, such as yoga. Qigong is described by the National Qigong Association on their website, *http://www.nqa.org*, as an "ancient Chinese health care system that integrates physical postures, breathing techniques and focused intention. The word Qigong is made up of two Chinese words. Qi is pronounced *chee* and is usually translated to mean the life force or vital-energy that flows through all things in the universe. The second word, Gong, pronounced *gung*, means accomplishment, or skill that is cultivated through steady practice. Together, Qigong (Chi Kung) means cultivating energy. . . ." Sample exercises of this mindful movement can be found on the Qigong Institute website, *https://www.qigonginstitute.org/category/58/sample-qigong-practices*.

What are ways you move physically in your life?

What are ways you have had to move emotionally along your path?

Are there ways you wish you could move emotionally, but feel stuck right now?

Ending

Prayer for Letting Go

Somehow a word, a thought, a memory
   crosses my heart
    and leaves a bruise.
The pain it causes is sometimes deep and
Lingers to color all my days.
Who can ease this pain that binds me?
I can—
By letting go.[1]

---

1. Joan L Huff, "Prayer for Letting Go," *Women's Uncommon Prayers: Our Lives Revealed, Nurtured, Celebrated*, ed. Elizabeth Rankin Geitz, Ann Smith, Marjorie A. Burke (Harrisburg, PA: Morehouse Publishing, 2000), 48.

Name

Definitions

Noun:

A word or set of words by which a person or thing is known, addressed, or referred to.

A famous person.

A reputation, especially a good one.

Verb:

Give a name to.

Identify correctly by name.

Give a particular title or epithet to.

Mention by name.

Appoint (someone) to a particular position or task.

Specify (a sum, time, or place) as something desired, suggested, or decided on.

Adjective:

Having a well-known name.

Beginning

What are words or thoughts that come to mind when you think of *name* or *naming*?

What is the history of your own *name*?

Genesis 48:16

". . . the angel who has redeemed me from all harm,
    bless the boys;
and in them let my name be perpetuated, and the name
    of my ancestors Abraham and Isaac;
and let them grow into a multitude on the earth."

Psalm 8:9

O Lord, our Sovereign,
    how majestic is your name in all the earth!

Isaiah 9:6

For a child has been born for us,
    a son given to us;
authority rests upon his shoulders;
    and he is named
Wonderful Counselor, Mighty God,
    Everlasting Father, Prince of Peace.

Luke 2:21

After eight days had passed, it was time to circumcise the child; and he was called Jesus, the name given by the angel before he was conceived in the womb.

ooo

O! be some other name:
What's in a name? that which we call a rose
By any other name would smell as sweet;
So Romeo would, were he not Romeo call'd,
Retain that dear perfection which he owes
Without that title. Romeo, doff thy name;
And for that name, which is no part of thee,
Take all myself.

—WILLIAM SHAKESPEARE, *ROMEO AND JULIET*,
ACT II, SCENE 2

PROCTOR: Because it is my name! Because I cannot have another in my life. Because I am not worth the dust on the feet of them that hang! How may I live without my name? I have given you my soul, leave me my name!

—ARTHUR MILLER, FROM *THE CRUCIBLE*, ACT 4

Words are things. You must be careful, careful about calling people out of their names, using racial pejoratives and sexual pejoratives and all that ignorance. Don't do that. Some day we'll be able to measure the power of words. I think they are things. They get on the walls. They get in your wallpaper. They get in your rugs, in your upholstery, and your clothes, and finally into you.

—MAYA ANGELOU, INTERVIEW WITH OPRAH WINFREY, *HTTPS://WWW.YOUTUBE.COM/WATCH?V=U7Y8FRS881K*

You Have Called Me by Name

Oh, Lord my God.
You called me from the sleep of nothingness
merely because in your tremendous love
you want to make good and beautiful beings.
You have called me by my name in my mother's womb.
You have given me breath and light and movement
and walked with me every moment of my existence.
I am amazed, Lord God of the universe,

that you attend to me and, more, cherish me.
Create in me the faithfulness that moves you,
and I will trust you and yearn for you all my days.
Amen.

—JOSEPH TETLOW, SJ (JESUIT)[1]

In the Bible, in both Greek Orthodox and Jewish traditions, names have utmost importance. Rabbi Berel Wein wrote on Torah.org, "For in our name lies our soul and self. That is why Jews always placed great emphasis on naming a child, for in that name there lay the history and past of the family and the hopes and blessings for the newborn's success—Jewish success—in life. I know of nothing that so deeply touches a family's nerve system as the naming of a child." (December 30, 2004)

Greek Orthodox blessing on the eighth day after birth:

O Lord our God, we entreat You, and we supplicate You, that the light of Your countenance be signed on this, Your servant, and that the Cross of Your Only-begotten Son be

1. Joseph Tetlow, SJ, "You Have Called Me by Name," in *Hearts on Fire: Praying with Jesuits*, ed. Michael Harter, SJ (Chestnut Hill, MA: Institute of Jesuit Sources, 1993), p. xx.

signed in her heart and understanding, so that she may flee from the vanity of the world and from every evil snare of the enemy, and may follow after Your commandments. And grant, O Lord, that Your holy name may remain unrejected by her, and that, in due time, she may be joined to Your Holy Church, and that she may be perfected by the dread Mysteries of Your Christ, so that, having lived according to Your commandments, and having preserved the seal unbroken, she may receive the blessedness of the elect in Your kingdom: By the grace and love for mankind of Your Only-begotten Son, with Whom You are blessed, together with Your Most-holy, Good, and Lifegiving Spirit, now and ever, and unto ages of ages.

> Are there ways, to echo Rabbi Wein's words, that you identify your soul, your self in *your* name?
>
> How has your name touched the "nerve system" of your family?
>
> Considering the Greek Orthodox naming prayer, are there ways you have rejected your name? If so, how did that rejection affect your view of yourself? If not, what kept you from ever rejecting your name?
>
> Are there ways you want to live more fully into any part of your name?

Ending

Being Known by God[2]

by Norvene Vest, Obl, O.S.B.

Begin by thinking of the many names you know for God: Lord, Creator, Jesus, Light, Mother, Father, Savior, Love, Abba, Bread, Thou and so forth. Decide on a particular name for this time, one that suggests the quality of God's presence you wish to call forth now. Repeat that name over and over softly to yourself for a minute or two, even moving your lips.

Continue saying God's name softly to yourself. To begin, think of what you know about the God who bears this name. Ponder all you know about God's essential being, and especially as One who chooses to be here for you now.

Continuing to say God's name, let your awareness of the name gradually sink down into the region near your heart. As you experience this passage, let go of your thoughts about God. Simply use the name as an arrow of longing cast forth from your heart toward God's heart. Don't think; just experience God's presence as the name repeats itself in your heart.

Allow yourself to be aware that this One in whose presence you are now enfolded knows you through and

2. From *Women's Uncommon Prayers: Our Lives Revealed, Nurtured, Celebrated*, ed. Elizabeth Rankin Geitz, Ann Smith, and Marjorie A. Burke (Harrisburg, PA: Morehouse Publishing, 200), 221–22.

through. What feelings does this awareness bring? Let the feelings come as they will, noticing them but not grasping them, so that they also go as they will, making room for whatever will come next.

Hear God say to you: "I delight in you. You are my beloved." Receive the truth and the empowerment of this reality as fully as you are able to right now. As you breathe in, take in God's word: "I love you." As you breathe out, give God your love. Continue this rhythmic breathing and loving for a time.

Rest peacefully in the quiet for some moments.

When you are ready, open your eyes and return fully to this now.

Amen.

Cairns

The "o" in the *Our One Word* logo evokes a cairn, reminding participants that their words and stories have the power to ripple through their communities and effect change. The original cairn was a Scottish Gaelic mound of rough stones used as either a memorial or to mark a sky or waterline. Enormous rock structures in Ireland date from around 4000 BCE. Today, the cairns most of us see and construct in nature are random stacks of progressively smaller—or larger, depending on how you look at it—stones along trails, in creeks, along rivers. I saw the other day, on someone's porch, a pumpkin cairn, bold striated orange and white on the bottom, teeny tiny orange on the top. Cairns invite questions: *Why did someone take the time to stack those rocks (or pumpkins)? How are the stones connected, separate? What is their ripple effect on the landscape, on me?* These are all questions we can also ask of the communities in which we exist.

Cairns are, as with most everything humans put their hands on, subjects of debate. Park rangers have long constructed these structures for hikers as a natural way, instead of a man-made sign, to mark the end of a trail. Hikers depend on certain cairns for safety, to know they are on the right path and have reached a particular spot. In the creek behind my parents' house, hikers, campers, prayerful folks constantly construct beautiful cairns on logs across the water, on large flat rocks within the water.

To some committed conservationists, this human manipulation of nature violates Leave No Trace principles, can cause erosion, and disrupts housing for animals and bugs. Robyn Martin, a lecturer at Northern Arizona University, calls these unofficial cairns "pointless reminders of human ego" akin to graffiti or trash (*http://www.npr .org/2015/08/05/429597208/making-mountains-out-of-trail -markers-cairns-spark-debate-in-southwest*). Others believe a cairn is a way to honor nature, a sign of community, an act of spirit. By creating or adding to a cairn, we signify we are thinking about those who walked before us, those who will follow.

Like a good Episcopalian, I see both sides. Sometimes we need to be in the woods so we remember God and forget for a moment all the imperfections and frailties of our humanness. I am frustrated when I see an empty Budweiser can along the trail or a boot-stomped orange mushroom. I want to know that the rocks and water and leaves are resting where they are supposed to be. At the same time, there is creative energy in the art of the cairn. The stacking makes me pay closer attention to the rocks themselves—the colors, the variations, the shapes, how they are similar, separate. When I see a cairn, I imagine someone's best intentions, their own care and exploration, their own quiet moments contemplating the stones. Imagining the best intentions of strangers is so foreign in our fearful culture that this exercise always surprises, delights me.

As much as I sometimes crave the illusion that no one else has walked a trail before me or waded in the cold creek where I'm standing, cairns remind me there is always someone before and there will always be someone after. Of course we must be responsible to nature and maintain Leave No Trace principles as much as possible. But I also wonder if, instead of resisting our communal belonging to and with each other, instead of insisting on standing as individuals, we could embrace the cairn as a symbol of the balanced, dysfunctional, beautiful, disappointing, joyful communities to which we all belong. An acknowledgment that we must, for our very survival, remain stacked, no matter how crooked sometimes, and present for each other.

Our immediate communities—our families, offices, and places of worship with whom we have some degree of shared blood, love, skill, or belief—can be challenging and difficult enough on their own, without even considering the groups of people who don't, God forbid, look like us or believe what we do. Even if we can breathe in some divine moments, all the opinions, divisiveness, and whining can scatter us to the wind, blow us right into our separate corners. Jesus, reversing all preconceived ideas about who is on top or who is at the bottom, instructs us to keep coming back to the circle. Even when it's not going like we think it should. Even when we have been hurt. Our communities are inevitable, critical to our survival and part of our Christian call, our human call. Jesus never said it would be easy.

M. Scott Peck, in his book *The Different Drum: Community Making and Peace*, writes:

> . . . there is a fantasy abroad. Simply stated, it goes like this: "If we can resolve our conflicts, then someday we shall be able to live together in community." Could it be that we have it totally backward? And that the real dream should be: "If we can live together in community, then someday we shall be able to resolve our conflicts?"

Talk about kicking the cairn, knocking down the predictable patterns. Our tendency when things get tough, which they always do, can be to escape, thinking we are better off on our own. Americans do this well. I do this well. *I can figure all this out without having to ask anyone. She/he/they will just make things difficult. If I didn't have to deal with her/him/them, everything would be fine and things would be manageable/easy/plentiful for me.* It is within this complex relationship with each other that we develop awareness of the reality, as heartbreaking as it can sometimes be, that everything is not about us. We can begin to ask the healthy, life-altering questions: *How am I making things difficult here? What is this person, this relationship, this group teaching me? How do I need to change for my own good, for the good of the world?* Or maybe, *How do I better need to define my boundaries? Should I walk away from this community? Is there anyone I need to forgive, including myself?*

God knows there are some relationships and communities that are not healthy and must be abandoned. We have all experienced at one time or another the painful realizations: *I can't take this job, this workplace anymore. This relationship or friendship is not life-giving anymore. I no longer feel at home in this church.* The decision to leave any community requires discernment about the reasons you want to leave. But I also believe it is not possible to resolve our individual weaknesses and corporate conflicts without the help of community members, even the pains in the asses. It is that moment, when we are most sure *we* are never pains, that God gets God's good laugh. The difficult people, our difficult moments help us define ourselves, our boundaries, our beliefs, and push us upward into growth, change, and action.

I wish I could say I always follow my own suggestions and everything works out just swell. It's easy for me to sit behind the safety of my computer screen and cast out some cairn-in-the-sky theories about community. Easy for me to walk through the woods by myself and contemplate joyfully stacking pretty stones and all getting along. These ideas about community can certainly evoke more questions than solutions. *What about those people who don't want to have a conversation with me? What about the groups that are openly hostile?* Jesus is not surprised by these difficult questions. He lived them, after all. But he kept walking, sometimes trudging, through the human chaos. Simple solutions and answers might bring some surface happiness, a minute of consolation, but they do not deliver the deep wisdom and authentic joy of the Holy Spirit.

Mark and I have moved thirteen times in twenty-eight years of marriage, so I have moved in and out of many communities—cities, towns, churches, schools, girls' sports teams, theater moms, graduate schools, writing groups, friend groups. The whole idea of who is in and who is out has always evoked intense emotion for me. The push-pull of it all: I want to stand alone, but I also need to be a part. Who belongs, who does not, what happens when conflict arises. Many times I have felt sure some groups I was trying to stick my toe into were already established, with no room for anyone new. I could not muster time and energy for other groups, which left me feeling guilty. It took me a while to figure out I was expecting too much perfection both from other people and myself. I started distilling questions I needed to ask of myself: *What do you need from this group? What ways are you/are you not willing to contribute? How is this community helping me to grow/causing me to wither?*

There are plenty of days when the only community I can manage—and sometimes even that is questionable—is the Community of Bourlakases. Five of us, all with unmet desires. Five of us who need to travel different paths. Five of us all hungry at the same time.

When I consider communities so radically different from ones I am familiar with, I get equally anxious and exhausted. *I don't understand the Muslim faith. I don't know what it's like to be brown, or black. I can't imagine how Native Americans feel.* I turn back to my squad of five, my family of origin, my comfortable friend group, and convince myself I can just put my energy there and everything will be fine. Let somebody else do the hard learning, the reconciliation.

This is the point at which the Christian narrative, the cairn on our path, stands tall. Within these challenging, forgiving, difficult, loving rocks of community we learn how to live. When we practice living in community with people who are different or marginalized or confusing, we begin to shift our view of ourselves and the world. We experience the authentic kingdom of God, the redemptive love of Christ in our own lives, and maybe, as Peck claims, begin to resolve our conflicts. There is no guarantee this connection will be life-giving, but we can at least open the space by offering our shared words, stories, experiences with each other. Then we reshuffle and adapt, even when we don't feel like it, because the adaptability itself provides energy and hope. We live, breathe, argue, and celebrate with those who embody both the fungi and the blooms of humanity.

My communities, even the close-knit ones with my most beloved people, are difficult at times. It is in the difficulty, the challenging, the talking—so *so* much talking—balanced with the card games and the laughter, that I learn the person God calls me to be, along with the person God does *not* call me to be. I need all of my groups, and the ones I do not yet know, for my sense of belonging, identity, meaning, purpose. Similarly, there are groups of people who need *me*: my questions, my kindnesses, my hope, my handshake, my eye contact, my concern, my food, my tears—our shared humanity. As much as I may pretend this is not the case sometimes, I have to remember I am not the beloved *only* child of God. I am one of a big ole family and I must keep hiking, even when there's no cairn, or too many, in sight.

The English artist Andy Goldsworthy, who creates site-specific art in the natural world, said, "There is life in a stone. Any stone that sits in a field or lies on a beach takes on the memory of that place. You can feel that stones have witnessed so many things."[1] Goldsworthy's vision of stones points to the interconnectedness of all of us. We each hold so many experiences, memories, and wisdom that need to be shared. Sometimes we are broad and mighty, balancing multiple rocks of all different varieties on our shoulders. Other times as we sit at the tip-top, awkwardly orange and fully exposed, in desperate need of the support below. We all teeter, wondering where I end and you begin, where we overlap, when we must extricate ourselves, when we must remain stacked. The way of the rock pile.

There is an old Scottish Gaelic blessing, a way of wishing someone health, wealth, and prosperity: "*Cuiridh miclach air do chàrn*," which translates, "I'll put

---

1. National Gallery of Art, *An Eye for Art: Focusing on Great Artists and Their Work* (Chicago: Chicago Review Press, 2013), 20.

a stone on your cairn." Our communities require interaction, addition, subtraction. They endure pelting rain, ice storms, and blinding sunshine. Sometimes they crash. But they are still works of art.

Bread

Heads—and butter—up! This session requires advance planning because you will want to *eat* bread while you *talk about* bread. If you do not bake bread, beg someone you know who finds bread-baking therapeutic to make a loaf, or seven, to share with each other. A perfect time for this session is a day close to Michaelmas, September 29, the Feast Day of St. Michael and All Angels.

Definitions

Noun:

Food made of flour, water, and yeast mixed together and baked.

The bread or wafer used in the Eucharist.

The food that one needs in order to live.

Informal:

Money.

Verb:

Coat (food) with breadcrumbs before cooking.

Phrases/Idioms:*

best (or greatest) thing since sliced bread

bread and circuses

- Entertainment or political policies used to keep the mass of people happy and docile.

bread and water

bread and wine

the bread of life

break bread

one cannot live by bread alone

one's daily bread

---

* I included common phrases/idioms with the definitions of *bread* because I think they are fascinating for conversation. Not every word we discuss has this many idioms. Which ones are your favorite? Do you know of others not listed here?

know which side one's bread is buttered (on)

take the bread out of (or from) people's mouths

want one's bread buttered on both sides

Matthew 26:26

While they were eating, Jesus took a loaf of bread, and after blessing it he broke it, gave it to the disciples, and said, "Take, eat; this is my body."

John 6:31

Our ancestors ate the manna in the wilderness; as it is written, "He gave them bread from heaven to eat."

John 6:58

"This is the bread that came down from heaven, not like that which your ancestors ate, and they died. But the one who eats this bread will live forever."

ooo

There are people in the world so hungry, that God cannot appear to them except in the form of bread.

—Mahatma Gandhi

If thou tastest a crust of bread, thou tastest all the stars and all the heavens.

—Robert Browning

Avoid those who don't like bread and children.

—Swiss Proverb

The smell of good bread baking, like the sound of lightly flowing water, is indescribable in its evocation of innocence and delight . . .

—M.F.K. Fisher, "How to Cook a Wolf," in *The Art of Eating*

Good bread is the most fundamentally satisfying of all foods; and good bread with fresh butter, the greatest of feasts.

—James Beard, *Beard on Bread*

Christ is both the one who feeds the 5000 with the food that perishes but sustains life *and* the bread that gives enduring life in the world. In Christ, both kinds of food are unified. The place of deprivation is reshaped. On this redefinition, the journey of the banquet hinges. The verbs of this invitation are only "come" and "believe."

—Cathy Campbell, *Stations of the Banquet*

The banquet, then and now, is celebrated in the midst of the empire. It is sandwiched between the realities of sin: our fractured relationships with each other, God, and creation. **This is the story of life in the midst of death, not in spite of death.** This banquet of wisdom is about the redemption and re-creation of the integrity of life. It is not an escape from life. It is not fantasy. It is a table prepared "in the presence of my enemies" (Psalm 23:5).

—CATHY CAMPBELL, *STATIONS OF THE BANQUET*

This may be my favorite quotation in this whole book, as it speaks to the right here-ness of our experience. What better proof of Christ in our midst—in *this* world—is there than the bread we break together?

The Feast Day of St. Michael and All Angels, or Michaelmas, is celebrated on or near September 29. Using the lessons appointed for the day (found in *Lesser Feasts and Fasts, 2006* or through various online lectionary sources), be like the ancient Celts and invite St. Michael, resident dragonslayer and protector of the harvest, to an *Our One Word* Michaelmas celebration. Scatter traditional Michaelmas daisies, or asters, or whatever you find in your yard or at Kroger, all over the table. Give thanks to God for the harvest of grain, the leaves, the illuminating darkness, the pumpkins, the introspective time, the candlelight, the hot chocolate, the holey blanket, the bean soup, the books, the butter, the wool socks, the fire. Break your bread and eat together.

Ending

We Try, As Best We Can, To Live By Bread Alone

We try, as best we can, to live by bread alone,
Or pie or cake or sweet rolls.
And then comes your word! In our hearing we are
    reminded that
We live by every word that proceeds from your mouth,
Promise and gifts,
Blessings and threats,
Summons and commands,
Assurances and requirements.
We thank you for bread, and for the many cakes, pies and
    sweet rolls

That inhabit our life of privilege. While we munch,

Give us ears, make us better listeners,

Give us patience with our odd utterances,

We vow to listen.

We pray in the name of your Son Jesus Christ who
became our bread.

Amen.

—WALTER BRUEGGEMANN,
AWED TO HEAVEN, ROOTED IN EARTH:
PRAYERS OF WALTER BRUEGGEMANN

Heaven

Definitions

Noun:

A place regarded in various religions as the abode of God (or the gods) and the angels, and of the good after death, often traditionally depicted as being above the sky.

God (or the gods).

A state of being eternally in the presence of God after death.

The sky, especially perceived as a vault in which the sun, moon, stars, and planets are situated.

A place, state, or experience of supreme bliss.

Phrases:

the heavens open

in seventh heaven

a match (or marriage) made in heaven

move heaven and earth to do something

stink (or smell) to high heaven

Beginning

Why even consider the meaning of *heaven*?

What words, emotions come to mind when you consider *heaven*?

The Episcopal Catechism, or Outline of Faith (found in the back of the Episcopal Book of Common Prayer), summarizes what Episcopalians mean by *heaven* and *hell*:

> Q. What do we mean by heaven and hell?
>
> A. By heaven, we mean eternal life in our enjoyment of God; by hell, we mean eternal death in our rejection of God.

How does this explanation work for you?

ooo

To see a World in a Grain of Sand
And a Heaven in a Wild Flower . . .

—WILLIAM BLAKE, *AUGURIES OF INNOCENCE*

We may be surprised at the people we find in heaven. God has a soft spot for sinners. His standards are quite low.

—DESMOND TUTU, *NO FUTURE WITHOUT FORGIVENESS*

The connections we make in the course of a life—maybe that's what heaven is.

—FRED ROGERS

Boughton says he has more ideas about heaven every day. He said, "Mainly I just think about the splendors of the world and multiply by two. I'd multiply by ten or twelve if I had the energy."

—MARILYNN ROBINSON, *GILEAD*

. . . there is a larger world behind the one we see around us every day. That larger world loves us more than we can possibly imagine, and it is watching us at every moment, hoping that we will see hints in the world around us that it is there.

—EBEN ALEXANDER, M.D., *THE MAP OF HEAVEN: HOW SCIENCE, RELIGION, AND ORDINARY PEOPLE ARE PROVING THE AFTERLIFE*

Jesus's resurrection is the beginning of God's new project not to snatch people away from earth to heaven but to colonize earth with the life of heaven. That, after all, is what the Lord's Prayer is about.

—N.T. WRIGHT, *SURPRISED BY HOPE: RETHINKING HEAVEN, THE RESURRECTION, AND THE MISSION OF THE CHURCH*

Heaven isn't, therefore, an escapist dream, to be held out as a carrot to make people better behaved; just as God isn't an absentee landlord who looks down from a great height to see what his tenants are doing and to tell them they mustn't. Heaven is the extra dimension, the God-dimension, of all our present reality; and the God who lives there is present to us, present with us, sharing our joys and our sorrows, longing as we are longing for the day when his whole creation, heaven and earth together, will perfectly reflect his love, his wisdom, his justice, and his peace.

—N.T. WRIGHT, SERMON AFTER ASCENSION, *FOLLOWING JESUS: BIBLICAL REFLECTIONS ON DISCIPLESHIP*

The New Testament says that when Christ does return, the dead will experience a whole new life: not just our soul, but our bodies. And finally, the location. At no point do the resurrection narratives in the four Gospels say, "Jesus has been raised, therefore we are all going to heaven." It says that Christ is coming here, to join together the heavens and the Earth in an act of new creation.

What the New Testament really says is God wants you to be a renewed human being helping him to renew his creation, and his resurrection was the opening bell. And when he returns to fulfill the plan, you won't be going up there to him, he'll be coming down here.

—N.T. WRIGHT, 2008 INTERVIEW
WITH *TIME* MAGAZINE

Write about or draw an aspect of your vision of *heaven*.

How do we see *heaven* in a wildflower?

What are ways we help God renew God's creation?

Ending

The Lord's Prayer

Our Father in heaven,
hallowed be your name,
Your kingdom come,
Your will be done,
on earth as in heaven.
Give us today our daily bread.
Forgive us our sins
as we forgive those who sin against us.
Lead us not into temptation
but deliver us from evil.
For the kingdom, power
and glory are yours
now and forever.
Amen.

Boundaries

Definitions

Noun:

A line which marks the limits of an area; a dividing line.

A limit of something abstract, especially a subject or sphere of activity.

A hit crossing the limits of the field, scoring four or six runs.

Beginning

Jeremiah 5:22

Do you not fear me? says the Lord;
  Do you not tremble before me?

I placed the sand as a boundary for the sea,
    a perpetual barrier that it cannot pass;
though the waves toss, they cannot prevail,
    though they roar, they cannot pass over it.

Proverbs 15:25

The Lord tears down the house of the proud,
    but maintains the widow's boundaries.

What is the significance of the Lord's defense of the widow's boundaries in this verse?

ooo

"No" is a complete sentence.

—ANNE LAMOTT

Compassionate people ask for what they need. They say no when they need to, and when they say yes, they mean it. They're compassionate because their boundaries keep them out of resentment.

—BRENÉ BROWN, *RISING STRONG*

There was a wall. It did not look important. It was built of uncut rocks roughly mortared. An adult could look right over it, and even a child could climb it. Where it crossed the roadway, instead of having a gate it degenerated into mere geometry, a line, an idea of boundary. But the idea was real. It was important. For seven generations there had been nothing in the world more important than that wall. Like all walls it was ambiguous, two-faced. What was inside it and what was outside it depended upon which side of it you were on.

—URSULA K. LE GUIN, *THE DISPOSSESSED*

Let's draw some boundaries. With pencils, markers, crayons—whatever helps you feel strong and confident—illustrate your important boundaries in these areas:

Love

Friendship

Food

Work

Religion/faith

Family

Are there times and places we should let our hearts be boundary-less?

When should we *not* hold too closely to our ideas of self?

Are there times your boundaries have failed you?

What are times you have been grateful for your boundaries?

Ending

Boundaries

Dust

Where do I stop and where
Do you begin? In the end
The dust of us all settles
In the cracks of well-walked paths.
It took God two days to create division—
Thunder clouds above
Stormy seas.
Even now I divide (like my father before);
Tiptoe the floor, leave last love unsaid.
Certain I do not feel as you who
Bears deep, aching feelings.

But I do—I am you.
Where does one season end and
New begin? Last leaf fall, first bloom burst—
Twilight blurring into night.
Where do I stop and where
Do you begin? In the end
The dust of us all settles.

—CONNOR B. GWIN
(WRITTEN FOR THIS BOOK)

Perfect

Definitions

Adjective:

Having all the required or desirable elements, qualities, or characteristics; as good as it is possible to be.

Free from any flaw or defect in condition or quality; faultless.

Precisely accurate; exact.

Highly suitable for someone or something; exactly right.

Thoroughly trained in or conversant with.

Absolute; complete (used for emphasis).

Mathematics:

(Of a number) equal to the sum of its positive divisors, e.g., the number 6, whose divisors (1, 2, 3) also add up to 6.

Grammar:

(Of a tense) denoting a completed action or a state or habitual action which began in the past. The perfect tense is formed in English with *have* or *has* and the past participle, as in they have eaten and they have been eating (present perfect), they had eaten (past perfect), and they will have eaten (future perfect).

Botany:

(Of a flower) having both stamens and carpels present and functional.

Denoting the stage or state of a fungus in which the sexually produced spores are formed.

Entomology:

(Of an insect) fully adult and (typically) winged.

Verb with object:

Make (something) completely free from faults or defects; make as good as possible.

Bring to completion; finish.

Satisfy the necessary conditions or requirements for the transfer of (a gift, title, etc.).

Beginning

What are words, thoughts that come to mind when you consider *perfect, perfection*?

What do culture and the world teach us about *perfection*?

Psalm 18:30

This God—his way is perfect;

> the promise of the Lord proves true;

> he is a shield for all who take refuge in him.

Matthew 5:43–48

"You have heard that it was said, 'You shall love your neighbor and hate your enemy.' But I say to you, Love your enemies and pray for those who persecute you, so that you may be children of your Father in heaven; for he makes his sun rise on the evil and on the good, and sends rain on the righteous and on the unrighteous. For if you love those who love you, what reward do you have? Do not even the tax collectors do the same? And if you greet only your brothers and sisters, what more are you doing than others? Do not even the Gentiles do the same? Be perfect, therefore, as your heavenly Father is perfect."

Romans 12:2

Do not be conformed to this world, but be transformed by the renewing of your minds, so that you may discern what is the will of God—what is good and acceptable and perfect.

2 Corinthians 12:9

. . . but he said to me, "My grace is sufficient for you, for power is made perfect in weakness." So, I will boast all the more gladly of my weaknesses, so that the power of Christ may dwell in me.

Colossians 3:14

Above all, clothe yourselves with love, which binds everything together in perfect harmony.

James 1:17

Every generous act of giving, with every perfect gift, is from above, coming down from the Father of lights, with whom there is no variation or shadow due to change.

1 John 4:12

No one has ever seen God; if we love one another, God lives in us, and his love is perfected in us.

ooo

Letting go of our prerequisites for worthiness means making the long walk from "What will people think?" to "I am enough." But, like all great journeys, this walk starts with one step, and the first step in the Wholehearted journey is practicing courage.

—Brené Brown, *The Gifts of Imperfection:*
Let Go of Who You Think You're Supposed
to Be and Embrace Who You Are

Whether you teach or live in the cloister or nurse the sick, whether you are in religion or out of it, married or single, no matter who you are or what you are, you are called to the summit of perfection: you are called to a deep interior life perhaps even to mystical prayer, and to pass the fruits of your contemplation on to others. And if you cannot do so by word, then by example.

Yet if this sublime fire of infused love burns in your soul, it will inevitably send forth throughout the Church and the world an influence more tremendous than could be estimated by the radius reached by words or by example.

—Thomas Merton, *The Seven Storey Mountain*

Too late, I found you can't wait to become perfect, you got to go out and fall down and get up with everybody else.

—Ray Bradbury, *Something Wicked This Way Comes*

Out of the crooked timber of humanity, no straight thing was ever made.

—AMELIE OKSENBERG RORTY AND JAMES SCHMIDT (EDS.),
QUOTING IMMANUEL KANT IN *KANT'S IDEA FOR A
UNIVERSAL HISTORY WITH A COSMOPOLITAN AIM*

List the words, ideas that arose for you from the quotations on *perfection*.

How does the idea of spiritual *perfection* differ from our worldly understanding?

With either words or a drawing, trace your winding journey both toward and away from *perfection*. Discuss with each other how this journey has shaped and will continue to form you.

What would you tell somebody ten, twenty years younger than you about what it means to be, and not be, *perfect*?

Ending

Canticle: A Song of True Motherhood

by Julian of Norwich

God chose to be our mother in all things *
and so made the foundation of his work,
    most humbly and most pure, in the Virgin's womb.
God, the perfect wisdom of all, *
arrayed himself in this humble place.
Christ came in our poor flesh *
to share a mother's care.
Our mothers bear us for pain and for death; *
our true mother, Jesus, bears us for joy and endless life.
Christ carried us within him in love and travail, *
until the full time of his passion.
And when all was completed and he had carried us
        so for joy, *
still all this could not satisfy the power of his wonderful
        love.
All that we owe is redeemed in truly loving God, *
for the love of Christ works in us;
Christ is the one whom we love.
Glory to the Father, and to the Son, and to the Holy Spirit: *
as it was in the beginning, is now, and will be forever.
        Amen.

Acceptance

May I remember, dear God, that I belong in your arms.

It is there that I am healed, and there that I am whole.

May all impurities be cast from my mind, my heart,
    my body.

May every fiber of my being be filled with your light.

May my cells vibrate with your divine energy.

May my body and soul radiate your love.

You are my divine physician.

In you I trust.

I accept your will for me.

I accept your healing.

I accept your love.

I accept myself.

Amen.

—GLENNA MAHONEY,
WOMEN'S UNCOMMON PRAYERS

Wilderness

Definitions

Noun:

An uncultivated, uninhabited, and inhospitable region.

A neglected or abandoned area.

A position of disfavor, especially in a political context.

Beginning

Describe the words, emotions that come to mind when you consider the word *wilderness.*

An important part of the definition is that the wilderness is considered "inhospitable."

As hospitality is a major theme of the Christian narrative, are there ways we are inhospitable to **ourselves** and to each other, creating unnecessary wildernesses?

There are about 287 references to wilderness in the Bible. In these stories, the wilderness, a place of testing and transformation, becomes an important character that cannot be avoided. It is not necessarily an evil place, but definitely not hospitable or friendly. We, along with the people of Exodus and our brother Jesus, are thrust into the wilderness where existence is demanding, difficult, sometimes doubtful. The relevance is striking. Always, when leaving the wilderness, people are transformed.

When reading our source quotations, hold in your mind and heart these questions:

What are the current personal, spiritual, social, political, or cultural wildernesses you face right now?

What emotions surface in a wilderness? What purpose do these emotions serve?

What are the tools you need for wilderness survival?

What survival skills do you already possess within you?

Maybe the Holy Spirit *wants* us to be in the wilderness at certain times. How does this perspective affect the way we view wilderness experiences, places?

Numbers 21:5

The people spoke against God and against Moses, "Why have you brought us up out of Egypt to die in the wilderness? For there is no food and no water, and we detest this miserable food."

Isaiah 35:6

[T]hen the lame shall leap like a deer, and the tongue of the speechless sing for joy. For waters shall break forth in the wilderness, and streams in the desert . . .

Matthew 4:1–11

Then Jesus was led up by the Spirit into the wilderness to be tempted by the devil. He fasted forty days and forty nights, and afterwards he was famished. The tempter came and said to him, "If you are the Son of God, command these stones to become loaves of bread." But he answered, "It is written, 'One does not live by bread alone, but by every word that comes from the mouth of God.'" Then the devil took him to the holy city and placed him on the pinnacle of the temple, saying to him, "If you are the Son of God, throw yourself down; for it is written, 'He will command his angels concerning you,' and 'On their hands they will bear you up, so that you will not dash your foot against a stone.'" Jesus said to him, "Again it is written, 'Do not put the Lord your God to the test.'" Again, the devil took him to a very high mountain and showed him all the kingdoms of the world and their splendor; and he said to him, "All these I will give you, if you will fall down and worship me." Jesus said to him, "Away with you, Satan! for it is written, 'Worship the Lord your God, and serve only him.'" Then the devil left him, and suddenly angels came and waited on him.

ooo

Thousands of tired, nerve-shaken, over-civilized people are beginning to find out that going to the mountains is going home; that wildness is a necessity; and that mountain parks and reservations are useful not only as fountains of timber and irrigating rivers, but as fountains of life.

—John Muir, *Our National Parks,* 1901, Introduction

Only by going alone in silence, without baggage, can one truly get into the heart of the wilderness. All other travel is mere dust and hotels and baggage and chatter.

—John Muir, letter to wife Louie, July 1888, *Life and Letters of John Muir* (1924), chapter 15

It is a lovely and terrible wilderness, such as wilderness as Christ and the prophets went out into; harshly and beautifully colored, broken and worn until its bones are exposed, its great sky without a smudge of taint from Technocracy, and in hidden corners and pockets under its cliffs the sudden poetry of springs.

—Wallace Stegner, *Wilderness Letter*,
Los Altos, CA, December 3, 1960

Anthropocentric as [the gardener] may be, he recognizes that he is dependent for his health and survival on many other forms of life, so he is careful to take their interests into account in whatever he does. He is in fact a wilderness advocate of a certain kind. It is when he respects and nurtures the wilderness of his soil and his plants that his garden seems to flourish most. Wildness, he has found, resides not only out there, but right here: in his soil, in his plants, even in himself . . .

—Michael Pollan, *Second Nature:*
A Gardener's Education, p. 192

It had to do with how it felt to be in the wild. With what it was like to walk for miles with no reason other than to witness the accumulation of trees and meadows, mountains and deserts, streams and rocks, rivers and grasses, sunrises and sunsets. The experience was powerful and fundamental. It seemed to me that it had always felt like this to be a human in the wild, and as long as the wild existed it would always feel this way.

—Cheryl Strayed, *Wild: From Lost to Found*
on the Pacific Crest Trail, p. 207

(Author's Note: I strongly recommend the book first, but Wild *is also a wonderful movie with Reese Witherspoon,* http://www.imdb.com/title/tt2305051/.)

There are two kinds of wilderness: the ones we are forced into and the ones of our own choosing. Both, as difficult as they may be, allow for transformation on small and grand scales. Cheryl Strayed thrust herself into the wilderness as a way of healing her body and soul.

> Using markers, crayons, or paints, draw or paint a picture of yourself in a wilderness you have faced. Be as detailed as possible. Study your picture when you are finished. What surprises you about your drawing? (Answer that does not count: "I am a terrible artist.")

Ending

Psalm 78

God split open the sea and let them pass through; *
making the waters stand up like walls.
Walls of chaos
Hover beside the Way
They railed against God and said, *
"Can God set a table in the wilderness?"
In deserts of loneliness
In wastelands of isolation
In rages of anger
In silence of apathy
Come, eat
The Bread is Broken for you.

—Women's Uncommon Prayers,
Lenten Prayer, p. 292

Surrender

Definitions

Verb:

Stop resisting to an enemy or opponent and submit to their authority.

(In sport) lose (a point, game, or advantage) to an opponent.

Give in to (a powerful emotion or influence).

Give up or hand over (a person, right, or possession), typically on compulsion or demand.

Give up (a lease) before its expiry.

Noun:

The action of surrendering to an opponent or powerful influence.

Beginning

What are the ways you understand the word *surrender* within our culture?

What are ways you understand *surrender* within a Christian context?

Where do the cultural and Christian meanings of *surrender* differ, converge?

Philippians 1:21

For to me, living is Christ and dying is gain.

Matthew 22:37

"He said to him, 'You shall love the Lord your God with all your heart, and with all your soul, and with all your mind.'"

Luke 9:23–24

Then he said to them all, "If any want to become my followers, let them deny themselves and take up their cross daily and follow me. For those who want to save their life will lose it, and those who lose their life for my sake will save it."

John 15:1–5

"I am the true vine, and my Father is the vine-grower. He removes every branch in me that bears no fruit. Every branch that bears fruit he prunes to make it bear more fruit. You have already been cleansed by the word that I have spoken to you. Abide in me as I abide in you. Just as the branch cannot bear fruit by itself unless it abides in the vine, neither can you unless you abide in me. I am the vine, you are the branches. Those who abide in me and I in them bear much fruit, because apart from me you can do nothing."

ooo

Surrender your own poverty and acknowledge your nothingness to the Lord. Whether you understand it or not, God loves you, is present in you, lives in you, dwells in you, calls you, saves you and offers you an understanding and compassion which are like nothing you have ever found in a book or heard in a sermon.

—THOMAS MERTON, *THE HIDDEN GROUND OF LOVE: THE LETTERS OF THOMAS MERTON*

Love is giving up control. It's surrendering the desire to control the other person. The two—love and controlling power over the other person—are mutually exclusive. If we are serious about loving someone, we have to surrender all the desires within us to manipulate the relationship.

—ROB BELL, *SEX GOD: EXPLORING THE ENDLESS CONNECTIONS BETWEEN SEXUALITY AND SPIRITUALITY*

I sometimes wonder whether the act of surrender is not one of the greatest of all—the highest. It is one of the [most] difficult of all . . . You see it's so immensely complicated. It needs real humility and at the same time, an absolute belief in one's own essential freedom. It is an act of faith. At the last moments, like all great acts, it is pure risk. This is true for me as a human being and as a writer. Dear Heaven, how hard it is to let go—to step into the blue.

—KATHERINE MANSFIELD, *THE COLLECTED LETTERS OF KATHERINE MANSFIELD*

At fifteen life had taught me undeniably that surrender, in its place, was as honorable as resistance, especially if one had no choice.

—MAYA ANGELOU, *I KNOW WHY THE CAGED BIRD SINGS*

Hymn: I Surrender All

Lyrics by Judson W. Van de Venter (1855-1939)

Music by Winfield Scott Weeden (1847-1908)

All to Jesus I surrender,
All to Him I freely give;
I will ever love and trust Him,
In His presence daily live. I surrender all,
    I surrender all.

All to Thee, my blessed Savior,
    I surrender all.

2

All to Jesus I surrender,
Humbly at His feet I bow;
Worldly pleasures all forsaken;
Take me, Jesus, take me now.

3

All to Jesus I surrender,
Make me, Savior, wholly Thine;
Let me feel Thy Holy Spirit,
Truly know that Thou art mine.

4

All to Jesus I surrender,
Lord, I give myself to Thee;
Fill me with Thy love and power,
Let Thy blessing fall on me.

5

All to Jesus I surrender,
Now I feel the sacred flame.

Oh, the joy of full salvation!
Glory, glory to His name!

From the above verses, quotations, and lyrics, list the words and phrases that stand out to you, scare you, surprise you. *Surrender* to a few moments of meditation on your list, then journal about one of the words or phrases. Consider how that word connects to the places and points of your life where you have or have not surrendered, maybe in a relationship or experience of your spiritual journey.

Ending

My Lord God, I have no idea where I am going. I do not see the road ahead of me. I cannot know for certain where it will end. Nor do I really know myself, and that I think I am following your will does not mean I am actually doing so. But I believe the desire to please you does in fact please you. And I hope I have that desire in all I am doing. I hope

I will never do anything apart from that desire. And I know if I do this you will lead me by the right road though I may know nothing about it. I will trust you always though I may seem to be lost and in the shadow of death. I will not fear, for you will never leave me to face my perils alone.

—FROM THOMAS MERTON'S *THOUGHTS IN SOLITUDE,*
PRAYER OF ABANDONMENT

Word

Definitions

Noun:

A single distinct meaningful element of speech or writing, used with others (or sometimes alone) to form a sentence and typically shown with a space on either side when written or printed.

Something spoken or written; a remark or statement.

Angry talk.

A command, password, or signal.

Communication; news.

One's account of the truth, especially when it differs from that of another person.

A promise or assurance.

Verb:

Express (something spoken or written) in particular words.

Origin:

Greek for *word* is *logos*:

The Word of God, or principle of divine reason and creative order.

Slang:

Basically means "truth." Or "to speak the truth."

Beginning

Considering the multitude of *word* definitions, what are ways words have come into your consciousness this week?

Are there words that angered or saddened you?

Are there words that lifted or illuminated you? Why?

What is your first memory of language?

What words keep you connected to God? To the people around you?

John 1:1

In the beginning was the Word, and the Word was with God, and the Word was God.

ooo

The plainest reason why the Son of God is called the Word, seems to be, that as our words explain our minds to others, so was the Son of God sent in order to reveal his Father's mind to the world.

—MATTHEW HENRY'S *CONCISE COMMENTARY ON THE WHOLE BIBLE*

It seems to me the perfect response to John 1:1 is *word*, in the slang sense. We don't need to look much further than this opening of John's Gospel to realize the importance of studying words and seeking spiritual strength within them. There is almost a birth within this verse, a familial movement from the Word existing alone, then with God, then becoming God.

> Are there significant words that have existed within you and come to define you during your life?
>
> Are there words you feel God has challenged you with, over your lifetime?

What are some of the cultural inventions meant to help us hold tension in a life-giving, not death-dealing way? Language itself is among the first of them, because it allows us to respond to tension with words instead of actions. . . . Language leads to the possibility of understanding, and thus to a true resolution of tension, something that is never achieved by fighting or fleeing, which merely leave more tension in their wake.

—WALLY LAMB, 3 WEAVINGS, XXIV: 2

Discuss or write your reflections on this beautiful passage by author Wally Lamb. While "language leads to the possibility of understanding," language and words can also be destructive, creating tension rather than resolving it.

> Do we have a Christian responsibility in our use of language and words with each other?

Ending

Let the words of my mouth and the meditation of my heart be acceptable to you, O Lord, my rock and my redeemer.

—PSALM 19:14

Stories

Here is a short story from an early feminist: "The kingdom of heaven is like yeast that a woman took and mixed in with three measures of flour until all of it was leavened" (Matthew 13:33). Like the lyric line of a song, we can memorize the entire story with a few punctuating downbeats: kingdom of heaven, yeast, woman, leaven. Within these twenty-five words is the entire purpose for and structure of *Our One Word*. The lesson, the understanding, the hope of the Gospel and of the world does not emerge from a winded old narrative, but from a crisp, fresh story about a bread-baking, female life. Through his stories, Jesus shares a bubbling new order, powered not by top-down dominance and control, but through wisdom, action, and love that permeates from within. A sugar-eating love and hospitality working to transform what is painful and hopeless into life-giving food.

If I put a voice to this woman-making-bread-dough story, I hear Jesus sounding fairly contained, pretty low-key. Not many words, no exclamation points, a little equation of yeast and flour. But my own voice erupts. *A woman! This story is about a woman!* In a time when women were considered powerless, sexual vessels and not much more, this evolved man narrates women right in the center of the story, right alongside the kingdom of heaven, turning all disrespect and old beliefs into something new. This bread-making female life is the one that will teach us about the Kingdom. Jesus's storytelling method is one we need—now more than ever—to study and practice in our flashy, opinionated culture. Now, more than ever. When anger and confusion permeate, these seemingly simple stories of hope and love flip us on our heads, point to the possibility of transformation, a different kind of life.

We are in desperate need of bread's crust (gluten-free included), that warmth, that butter. But bread, like all good things, requires thought and effort. We have to consider whether and how this method of story-sharing carries water in our own culture, so different from that of Jesus's time. Rest assured, as long as there is conflict, desperation, and anxiety, there is need for and value in sharing our stories with each other. Humans, in their sometimes-smartness, can even prove it.

One of the foremost story researchers, psychologist Sherry Hamby, director of the Life Paths Appalachian Research Center (LPARC), co-chair of ResilienceCon, and research professor of psychology at the University of the South, writes,

> There are few interventions more powerful than sharing stories—and few with as much scientific evidence to support them. Telling your story allows one to process and, if needed, reframe events. Narrative helps people acknowledge their past, without letting past adversities define them. Putting your experiences into story format is great for achieving a sense of perspective and can help promote post-traumatic growth.[1]

Even if there is not a specific trauma in your life, sharing our narratives frees us from dwelling too much in past difficulty. We are empowered to define our lives by our resilience, our new potential, our new narratives.

In a 2008 study at Emory University, Drs. Duke and Fivush concluded from their research with children and teens, "Knowledge of family history is significantly

---

1. Personal correspondence with author.

correlated with internal locus of control, higher self-esteem, better family functioning, greater family cohesiveness, lower levels of anxiety, and lower incidence of behavior problems."[2] Their research goes on to specify that the most beneficial family stories focus on themes of resilience and survival. For example, instead of just imparting, *Our family has always been financially secure,* it's helpful to share the full story: *After the stock market crash, our grandparents lost everything. They had to sell their house and start again from scratch. Because of that history, we have focused on what's truly important to us and worked to establish more financial security for our family.*

We smarty-pants adults know this wisdom does not just apply to children or teenagers. Most everyone is bolstered by stories of resilience both within and outside of our families of origin. We don't buy a $12 ticket to sit through movie after movie, or read novel after novel, of a character's easy path to success. We want to read about and see on the screen characters who rise above difficult circumstances, overcome adversity, and transform themselves into changed, better people.

As with many parents who overshare about their incredible kids (I see your rolling eyes), I can be repetitive

---

2. Marshall P. Duke, Amber Lazarus, and Robyn Fivush, "Knowledge of Family History as a Clinically Useful Index of Psychological Well-Being and Prognosis: A Brief Report," *Psychotherapy* 45 (2008): 268–72, 10.1037/0033-3204.45.2.268.

and annoying when I talk about our oldest daughter Hannah who has autism. After about twenty-two years, I hope I am less annoying than I used to be. I spent too much time making sure people knew I had a daughter with disabilities, instead of just talking, laughing, crying about my wonderful child. With God's help, I have intentionally worked on moving from a story focused on Hannah's loss, my loss, to a story of abundance, joy, gratitude. Hannah's and my story is far from complete and perfect, as it requires daily, sometimes moment-by-moment rewriting and editing, but it is, in our best moments, open and hopeful.

When Hannah was born and later diagnosed with developmental disabilities, I created for myself a story of scarcity. I must have something less-than in my body to have produced a child with disabilities. I must not have done enough for her, worked hard enough to help her. Hannah was difficult, needy, sometimes scary. I must not have given her enough puzzles, enough gluten-free snacks. If I had, both of us would not have struggled. I did not have enough love, enough patience, enough knowledge, enough hope, enough kindness to be the mother of Hannah.

Not knowing many other mothers of children with disabilities, especially daughters, I kept all my guilt and shame to myself, for fear of how mothers of neuro-typical children and anybody else would judge me. I composed words and thoughts for all those unnamed people in the world who had nothing better to do than observe my mothering. *How can she not control her child in the grocery store? All she has to do is love that poor child more and she will be fine.* My anxiety and sadness peaked, the more I became the story I told.

Creating a new narrative was a gradual process, with the help of many wise souls, but I remember a distinct moment. I was sitting with a mug of hot tea in my therapist's office and she said to me, "Martha, people look into Hannah's eyes and know what they need to know. You don't have to convince everyone she is one way or another. They know she is Hannah." After hearing these words, I realized how I had been trying to coerce people into believing what I thought Hannah was and was not. I focused on the skills and abilities Hannah lacked instead of focusing on everything she brings to the world. I wanted people to understand how we were both suffering. In my narrow view of what intellect, simplicity, pain, learning, prayer, and joy all truly meant, I was trying to over-control both Hannah's and my own stories. We both needed a liberating gospel.

At this same time, I began praying differently. I had always been a dutiful Christian—doing, doing—but now I was worn out. Instead of trying to direct God, I needed just to listen for the Holy Spirit's presence in my life. I started hearing Jesus's stories differently. Instead of hearing the words *shame* and *judgment*, I started hearing *grace* and *forgiveness* and *light*. Instead of constantly enumerating Hannah's *deficits* and *weaknesses*, I started attending to her *emotional awareness*, her *connectivity with people*, her *spiritual strengths*. Adopting new words allowed us both a new, less bitter, more hospitable narrative.

This softening enabled me to let my guard down so I could listen and talk to more mothers, grandmothers, aunts, friends. The more we shared, the more we had in common, whether or not they had children with disabilities. All different kinds of stories. Over and over. *I am caring for my father with Alzheimer's. I just received a cancer diagnosis. My husband left me for my best friend.* When we can hear *Hey, that happened to me too* or *I understand exactly the way you feel*, both storyteller and listener become empowered, more hopeful, able to move forward with the understanding *I am not alone*.

Many of the stories I have heard over the past few years of leading *Our One Word* sessions and workshops have blown me right off course, changed me forever. Like the woman who waited till the end of our weekend together, her face wide open with courage, and asked to share the story of her son who has been in a wheelchair since a young age and the two kinds of cancer she had survived. All of us listened, nearly shocked into silence by her perseverance, her ability still to laugh, her wisdom, the fact that her hair looked perfect. All of these stories are part of the narrative God calls us to compile, staple together if we must, and keep reading, writing, and sharing.

One of the most beautiful expressions of the power of telling stories, either verbally or written, is from a February 2008 *O Magazine* interview with author Wally Lamb about the writing workshops he leads with incarcerated women. Lamb says, "The rehabilitative power of our words invites us to test our still-wet wings, tentatively at first and then with greater and greater assurance. And as that happens, we rise above the concrete and razor wire of painful memories, baffling personal mysteries, and imprisoning secrets. Our load lightens, our perspective changes. We fly away." I pray that the words of this book and the stories you share with each other will lighten your load, open the hospitality of your soul, and enable you to fly away.